GALOS; Z J

SHORT STORIES
PART ONE
BOOK I & BOOK II

BOOK I
MY WRITING TOOLS
From a Writer's Workshop

BOOK II
FANTASTIC JOURNEYS
The Flight of Fantasy

Impressum

Bibliographical information of the German National Library

The German National Library indexes this publication with the German National Bibliography .Detailed bibliographical data may be derived from the Internet website http://dnb.dnb.de

Producer and publisher: BoD-Books on Demand, Norderstedt.

ISBN: 9783751958769

Contents

Book I

Book II

BOOK I

MY WRITING TOOLS

Fire into my Heart

The morning stirred with one sharp warble of a hopeful tit. I woke and nursed my erection. Then I proceeded to slide out between the sheets to walk to the bathroom. Two steps down behind the red-flowered linen curtains I touched my penis. It felt still strong and virile. I thought of washing my face, but that would wake me, I gathered, and walked back through the thick bi-parted curtains, went straight back to bed and tucked below the warmth of the covers, and I carried on with my dream. In the warmth of a sun-filled beach I stretched upon the well-heated soft sand. The sun warmed, but did not burn me, seducing my skin to pleasurable delights and I desired this image: Myrto. She appeared out of the blue. A young Venus, born from the crest of the sea. She approached me.

"I am Myrto," placing herself close-by to where I lay.

"Nice meeting you," I said, "I like your name."

"Thank you," she replied and smiled, promises sparkling from her eyes.

"Your name reminds me of a myrtle reef placed upon a winning poet's head," I said.

"Are you a poet?" She exclaimed. Her eyes opened wide.

"I am to be. At times I feel I am, at other times I do not feel at all that I am one." I replied.

"But then we all are not sure about who we are," she said walking to the beach close by and embracing the mist of the sea that dissipated into her sheer cotton clothes. The sun rose on the horizon, burning the dissipating mist and her clothes disappeared against her youthful glare. I saw her feet's parted stance with the sensual curves of her svelte body I gazed at.

"You are dreaming?" She queried, "…about me?"

"Yes," I said, "I saw you being born from the crest of the gentle morning waves, floating to this forlorn beach and inverted lagoon, your cotton clothes fired to ashes by the sun."

"I can take them off for you," she said.

"You excite me, Myrto, like the penetrating warmth of the rising sun..." She peeled her top off and then her skirt, wound on her bums in layers.

"Hold on to this end," she gasped and turned like a spindle uncoiling from the wound-on layers of sheer cotton. Like a mummy, I thought, coming unwound to be alive. With every one of her turns my heartbeat increased. I felt my chest rise and fall faster, still I tried holding my breath.

"What happened to you Zane?" A voice said. I opened my eyes and looked into Melanie's face. "Myrto...?" I murmured. She had brown eyes like Myrto. I followed her high cheek bones to her beautifully sculpted lips, and down her slender neck, close to me, as she bent down.

"No," she said, "I'm Tiff, your facilitator." She smiled with a strange expression examining me like a medical doctor, concerned about my state of health. She was glad I showed vital signs of life.

"You must have dreamed, as you talked aloud," she quipped. I felt ashamed.

"I always dream Mela... – Tiff," I replied faster showing her my attention level to be intact.

"All I've asked from you, was to write a scene about a holiday experience," she said.

"Yes, " I said, "I woke up this morning and the air felt fresh, the pallid skies reminded me of the sea and the mist of her dress that turned transparent against the sun..."

"That sounds beautiful," she exclaimed, "a well described scene, but now find the needle in the haystack!" She smiled.

"AH!" I cried out, "I sat on one already." Tiff laughed and I joined her. I just worked away the rules of editing, she had installed in me in these hours of editing closeness.

She leaned back, her auburn hair fell to her shoulders and she closed her eyes. Her high cheek-boned face reminded me of Myrto, yet the paleness of her skin gave her away as Tiff, against Myrto's olive taint. She sat in her workshop's chair concentrating on her soldering work as silver smith, while Tiff taught us to become successful word smiths. We sat at her feet admiring her as a goddess of words, while Myrto's girlfriend sat wide-legged on a stool at her feet, absorbing her like a spider, spinning around her a cocoon to soften her up for a luscious meal.

I started to sweat. The blond German amazon was about to lance her like a vulnerable deer. She had shot her arrows towards me, but the Goddess of Love had made them to miss me. In the first round of battle I was lucky and safe. I disliked the amazon, but good education demanded me to control my antipathies. Instead I called upon Apollo to provide me with an advantage in the war of words, in an ensuing discussion that turned into a dispute about the Holocaust.

Myrto, the artist, silversmith and sensual woman had turned into a facilitator to smooth over historical matters of a great tragedy that her blond amazon-friend had misinterpreted, showing a racist attitude. I won the argument morally, with Myrto standing next to me, and her nearness turned me tender towards her. It was after all her life, and I was her customer. I had no right barging into it.

But I also knew that this day belonged to them and the amazon was greedy for her, without any intention to include me into their love games at all.

I left with a sweet taste of acceptance by Myrto, into which a bitter after taste of her amazon friend's refusal blended into. Myrto called after me to come and see her tomorrow again. I did not turn around, hurt and misunderstood; I had still enough love to give, yet not waste energy on senseless talk. Stupid cows, what have they thought of doing with their intentions? Imagine, making love to such a fire and ice mixture. Perhaps the amazon woman plays rough in bed too? Yet, who would think of a blond woman behaving like that?

"Your writing has improved," Amara said and I felt a surge of pride, forwarding a message about it to Anna.

She was the friend who wanted me to visit a writing class, all the time we talked about literature and writing. She reminded me to learn proper sentence structures and only once I knew the rules I may change them, not before.

I used to laugh at her, an artist falling in love with her at such an ease, pulling her leg, making fun, painting the town's Acropolis red. But slowly her words sunk into the garden of my conscious mind and grew, like seeds she once planted into its fertile imaginary ground.

"You have to visit one of the grammar courses," Amara said, "if you want to become a professional writer." Again the seeds of Anna reared their heads and the green shoots started growing.

"I recall your quotations of Gertrude Stein on Hemingway, changing from a journalist to a Nobel Laureate writer." I said and nodded and booked immediately a course. I thought of Anna and Myrto. Now, as I stood in front of Myrto, like once before Anna, my heart my heart spoke immediately to her. Feelings poured from me forth. I sensed the vibrations in her slim body responding to my longing to touch her intimately.

Amazon-Grete drove not only a wedge between our intimate and delicate bond, I offered to Myrto, but she intercepted the palms of Myrto's hands holding my heart, where it had melted into a ball of silver she closed her fingers around, and Myrto just tucked it in time into one of her drawers. She would work on it later, alone, recall the warm glow she had extended to me, and shape it back into a heart again. She wanted me to fetch it and share her wondrous creation with her alone. But Grete's attack foiled the attempt and it fell to the stone floor and broke into two pieces. The torch of Myrto's sensual being cut into my flesh and I cried out. The pain of being torched with the scent of burning flesh is as abhorrent as Grete's endeavour to turn me to ashes. But she failed to cut me off from Myrto's feminine side, as Myrto tried fitting together the pieces. Like Isis, she descended to the underworld to summon the help of Toth. Finally, she claimed joyfully to have finished and the Gods gave me back my life. It was all there and even Grete wished to destroy my penis, it was still stuck onto my body, all right. Cast aside by this unexpected turn of fate, I made an enemy only defending myself.

I collapsed on the beach outside. I felt Myrto's kisses that the gentle sea lapped at my feet. I could not take the sea and my swim that afternoon. The weight of my emotions became lead of a fishing tackle that sank to the bottom of 'The Blue', in an attempt to drown and end the pain of longing, want, and sorrow. I knew I wanted Myrto and it would take time to enjoy her in peace and in love. The day of choice had to be right. Right in colour upon hues in the shrubs around, the olive trees, the buildings, and the beach. The colour of the sky and the sea with the correct amount of clouds that formed a harmony, if one is to become sensitive to sounds, light, and the scents of her island. The right type of clothes, in the right colours, we need to wait for the magic moment, when the sun burns our clothes and our skin will heat by the touches of our bodies to become one with the land, the sea, the clouds as the gift of god's universe, means the gift of love.

"Daydreaming again Zano?" She said and looked at me with enquiring eyes that still showed at times traces of her myopic state, she carried along like a burden on her back. She was in pain.

"I have finished my scene," I said and handed Melanie...-sorry, Tiff, the paper.

"I will comment on it this afternoon," she said. "I'll send you E-mail." She concluded.

"Thank you," I replied and then woke up in bed. It was already late morning and all the time I did recall that I wrote some poems for Myrto this morning. It came to me like a flash of lightning out of the blue, striking the elongated island of olives, sending its fire into my heart.

*

High Speed Sex.

Helen felt tricked by her mind. Pictures of Susan and her appeared on the huge Plasma screen in the Disco dancing hall. She gazed upon her lover's slim body sliding like a lizard upon hers. She never felt uneasy about gender sex, but this time a deep inner embarrassment started from her belly growing into a monster.

When the monster's vile tentacles strangled her throat, she rose, apologized to the group of dancers, and tried to collect herself. Her feet steadied. She put this attack down to her tiredness of city life, overwork, and the stress of late nights with Susan, 'The Lizard'.

"Are you all right Helen?" Susan spoke to her, but she perceived her voice as if from a distance.

"Yes. I'm fine. I just remembered that I have to be at a book-signing event later..." She replied without looking back at the table of celebrating literati.

Maurice rose. "I'll take you to your car." His dark looks emphasized through his black eyes.

"Thanks," she stammered at this unexpected courtesy, but forewarned by her sixth sense. His dark eyes – impossible to read – he never gave away his feelings, Helen thought. But this couldn't be Maurice, the man with a limp, as she remembered him. At the Paris dance studio, he gave lessons in Latin American dancing styles. Since then matters had changed. The break-up had been traumatic...Maurice touched her arm and her body reacted. It cannot be, she thought, I never loved him but his trained body.

Her mind seemed muddled. Pictures of their lovemaking mixed with Susan's way of loving her. She blamed that on the champagne. Impossible. The light-headedness came and left like a lapping of waves.

"Take my car, Helen, I know you are a good driver," he said and stopped at his new silver-blue sports Merc 500.

"Your new car?" She gasped.

"I had it delivered two days ago, for the start of my forth-coming dancing tour."

"It's impressive!" She stroked the soft, light-grey leather seat and Maurice handed her the keys. She hesitated at first, but then she couldn't resist driving the sleek mechanical messenger of the Gizmo-gods.

"It's a great toy, isn't it?" She heard a voice far away and it wasn't related to Maurice. She had not even noticed that he had joined her.

"Wow," she gasped, as the sleek Merc pulled from the curb like a rocket launch. She had fallen for the gleaming, seductive toy, and the instant acceleration aroused her. She wondered what on earth had happened to her in the last few hours. Her light-headedness had worsened, but she felt to be still in control. Her mind raced to Susan, who, she thought, sat next to her. How wonderful. She would give her a scare, and frightened, she would cuddle up in her lap.

"Woooeee – "She cried out and floored the accelerator. "Not so fast, Helen!" Susan's voice trembled and she enjoyed this instant power over her girlfriend.

"I will break the speed record along this motorway for tipsy women," she laughed huskily. The top button of her taught dress opened up as she yanked the fifth gear into position. Maurice slipped his hand on her. "You have warm fingers, Susan," Helen cried out as he opened the buttons on her dress. Helen's half-cups enticed Maurice to touch her hardened nipples. She sighed as he opened the front and her breasts popped free. "Uhhgg," she gasped. "Uhhgg! You want to make love to me at high speed?" Her nipples hardened to his touches. "I hardly know you Susan, but are you up to it?"

Maurice kept still as he slid his hand down her body. All buttons opened, he placed his lips on her and sucked her nipple, while his fingers played on her vulva. "Uhhgg!" She cried out, hit by an electric current. She swerved the car as he opened up her legs. "Oh Susan…not so fast…but I like it!" The moment he stroked her clit, an electric wire raced through her body…with a flash she came to her senses. "NO!" She shouted, "YOU ARE MAURICE! GET YOUR HANDS OFF ME!" He fell over her like lichen and his vile fingers dug into her pussy. "GET OFF NOW YOU BASTARD!" She yelled, pushing his hand with her one hand aside. Her leg jerked up hitting his forehead. He fell to the side as the Merc reeled over to the oncoming traffic lane. Helen pulled the car back and it skidded along the barrier rail and it skinned the car's side. Then, in her rage, she lost control – "you have the face of a devil," she cried out as the Merc bolted through a gap in the rails and skidded down an embankment, and then jumped like a mountain goat. It rolled three times on undulated soft ground and pushed along green fields, crashing into a low natural boundary wall, stones flying in all directions.

Helen turned instantly sober and she took Maurice's knife from its halter underneath his tee-shirt and cut the blocked seatbelts. It smelled of petrol and heat. She wrestled herself loose and wanted to get up, but her left leg gave in and she collapsed. As she tried to get up again, she hopped to the other side of the car to help Maurice, but he had disappeared.

She took a broken twig she found nearby and supported her leg, she could not step on. She searched for her handbag and found it near the car. She took Maurice's knife and hopped from the smelling debris toward the motorway. She needed distance from it as she feared it'll soon catch fire. By the time she had reached the motorway the car had caught fire and she sat down at the embankment to dial Susan's number on her mobile phone. At that moment the car exploded with a bang. She moved up the embankment and leaned against the barrier rail. A fire engine's whining sounded as Susan answered her call. "It's me, Helen…we had an accident…please come!" Susan would be able to trace her, as she left the connection open. "Damned Maurice," she thought "I bet the car is not registered in his name. That's why he disappeared in such a flash." She found a storm water manhole near the adjacent flyover bridge and threw the knife into it.

Susan appeared with her maroon Vauxhall. The car suited her auburn looks. "Helen! Thanks god you are alive!" She hugged her and they kissed. "Susan, get me to M's private clinic fast." Susan got Helen seated in the back of her old-timer Vauxhall and Helen could stretch her leg comfortably on the leather seat. It hurt her as she adjusted it and she knew it was broken. Susan handed her a pill box and a water bottle. "Painkillers," she said and handed her a water bottle from the mini-bar, her 'Vauxhi' had installed.

"Thanks darling," Helen cooed. "I love you."

"I love you too, Helen," Sue replied and added "no more adventures with guys like that!" Helen mumbled agreement, but she started dozing off, as the strong painkillers had a tranquilizing effect on her."...I thought I was driving ...with you...next to me..." she murmured.

"Oh did you feel threatened?" Susan said.

"Yes...when he...touched me...and I realized it was ...not you." Susan smiled, the emergency lane of M's private clinic appeared. "Stay with me...Susan". Helen whispered, as she was placed on a stretcher. "Yes, I will love." She replied and Helen blew her a kiss. She responded pressing her hand. Helen disappeared into the examination bay.

*

Julia and her Spirit

I had signed-up for a course in writing. It took me one year from having hatched the idea, having read an advertisement, to get finally through to the registration office.

"What are you here for?" The luxuriant woman asked and I felt as if she would undress me in front of many women bystanders. "I am here to know more about writing in the romantic genre." I said. Was she to eat me or spank me? I wasn't sure. Her facial expression did hardly change and she was not moving differently to her steady daily routine.

"Have some coffee," she said, "it's next door." I went through the door of an annexed room and to the right, two steps up to a higher, but smaller area, there was a kitchen sink and some cupboards. At two high tables snacks were laid out. At one table some cookies, at the other one creamy marmalade scones. I passed both.

I took to the brown liquid in the Pyrex bottle that sat on a hot plate. The coffee smelled good, but I couldn't handle the round and generous mouth of the bottle pouring coffee into a tiny cup. Short, I made a mess of it. The coffee swapped past the pouring lips onto my saucer and passed it. I felt ashamed. There was only one young woman seated on a high stool in the corner, and she did not observe me. Another woman entered and talked to the seated person with her back towards me. I thought of cleaning the stone floor, but there was no kitchen paper handy. So I assured myself that the spot of spilled coffee will soon evaporate from the dark stone surface, besides it wasn't blatantly visible.

As soon as the wide-hipped woman passed me to have coffee, I stepped over to talk to the young woman and asked her about her writing. As she talked I observed the wide-hipped woman pouring coffee, and she had the same problem as I had, spilling some on the stone floor. She was making a noise about it and I had to laugh inside.

The young woman told me that she was a poet. What type, I wanted to know. More women rushed suddenly in to have a cuppa, and there was no reasonable conversation possible any longer with her. Now what?

Then she stood suddenly in the middle of the room, laughing and conversing with the poetess I had talked to. Her face reminded me of an actress I had fancied in one of the romantic movies. As she looked into my direction I asked her a question about coming here. "We came four years ago," she said. "Obviously difficult to make friends, we have started a family." She carried on with the poetess and talked about her likings. I sipped my coffee and listened. She had turned to creative writing as her domain, yet she was seeking a social club of writers, who met at occasions like this, have an exchange of ideas, review books, and start writing a book once the inspiration had captured her fancy, and she had chosen a genre she liked.

For me it was all new, electrified by the atmosphere of many writers in one spot, I had immediately an idea what to write. I wanted to write something about my life, something gripping from reality. "Wrong," the facilitator said. "Don't write about your life. This is romantic fiction writing," she hammered on. "What about inner dialogues?"

"No, we don't have that here," she answered. And now overwhelmed by the talkative woman, who had arrived four years ago, I watched her dusky eyes glow as she talked. While she expressed her thoughts in immaculate English, her smile showed her joy with a tinge of sorrow and pain, all writers are subjected to in their solitary art. I had an interest to know more about her, but the luxuriant lady at reception came to announce the start of the course at the inner sanctum of a conference room, along a table that seated twelve persons.

"I am Nat," the course facilitator announced. Everybody introduced themselves with their name and the reason to be here. I was the only man, and immediately Apollo came to mind, who was surrounded at least by nine, or perhaps even ten Muses. Here we had perhaps ten Muses, besides the two extreme feminist women, who were disfigured by overeating; besides, I never fancied their writing they read to us. So, down to ten. – Fine with me. Apollo remained indifferent. This is not intended to be a countdown at a beauty contest. This is a personal selection with a quick test for personalities and their angle of view on romance, I thought, cutting loose the blond flirtatious woman, well – nine.

The petite woman next to me fades away and I cannot, for the best of my abilities, give her more than four out of ten. I'm sorry dear – eight.

How do I know I fare among the crowd of women exhibitionists? There would be no more than two or three who'd talk to me, expressing their curious interest in the only man, or even in his romantic scenes he writes.

"Do you like Coetzee?" I ask the young, sturdy woman with big boobs next to me on the right.

"I prefer Brink," she said, busying herself with her text. She is rather distinct with her voice. I think of her not as a Muse for myself. Ouch – seven are left. I look at the next writer, reading her story. Well, rather dull – six.

There she is, pale as bone china, without a blemish on her skin. The luminous face evaporated from the book she writes, stirring the fire in my belly. I feel that way as I read my own scene, her eyes on me; an inner force drives me into euphoric excitement. She's watching me, I thought. My God! My fingers on her thigh, as if I sat next to her, I swear. She smiled and commented on my thought of bringing some roses, and the way she'd close the door, if I would come and see her.

And now it's her turn to tell me what she'll do. And I hear her talking to meet me, causing another stir in my belly, and I wish I could be with her somewhere more private than in a round table session with all these aspirant novelists. However, soon I do not see anybody else but her, and I'm rather tactful avoiding to stare at her. I look at her with stolen glances, long enough, to study her Patrician nose. AyAy floats in front of my mind's eyes. I compare their profiles and they match. In my innerness a joyful pain, a stab. I want to cry. The voice tells me: It's me, AyAy. No! It cannot be, I never believed in reincarnation. But, who knows? In love it may count.

Whatever, hocus-pocus or not, I am bewitched by the thought and the start of a basic comparison, as this fiery Phoenix takes a flight – AyAy rising from the ashes and turning suddenly into Julia.

At last, I think, I do not have to seek my Muse in future. Then, as all sudden revelation succumbs like a climax and the storm of emotion settles into the next recommended action, I sense the tempest: Fools rush in.

This is it; she says inside me, you are smitten. Don't you feel well and are fond of me looking at Julia? You are in love, aren't you? I do not answer directly, walk towards the bookshelf and take a book on offer for a review. The worst I could choose, just due to Julia standing next to me. I swim like a lark in the presence of her eyes that wash away the pain in my heart.

I am too shy to ask her for a meeting, an E-mail address, or he mobile phone number, or a space she could suggest where I could meet her. It would be heaven, or it could be hell. It could be both. My mind runs the track of a circle and I run forward, too scared to face the endearment offered by the God of writing, who is partnered ny the Goddess of love.

And even if I run away from my feelings, there is no way all will evaporate into Gauteng's oily air. I cannot forget her face, the way she talks and carries her smile, reminding me of an avenging angel. Dark and southern, she lobs my heart high into the poet's air and then she catches it like a tightly dressed acrobat.

I sigh as I drive and think of many words that come to me. I park my car, walk across to my room and place myself into my favourite chair, taking my notebook with Klimt's flowers on the cover. I write her a poem as fast as I can. How could I ever hand her any note? I have missed to note down her E-mail, darned! Now it's up to the Gods to arrange another meeting. I want it, want it strong, and then again I don't want it, place a headphone on my ears and turn Keith Jarrett's music on loud, drowning my true feelings. Shit! This won't work now and it never will. I'll write her some words of love and it becomes another poem. Jesus! This is the strongest longing I had for a woman, since AyAy's death. I counted twenty months since. She had told me since to move on to another stealthy love. I'll do just that.

I met Julia at Erwin's, another book signing event. She was here due to Santa, a famous romance writer. I observe her profile at a table to the right, just in front of me. Suddenly I decide to move and get a book signed by Santa, but Julia beat me to it, she is ahead of me. I follow. We talk, she is all for a friendly chat. She talks at the same time to Santa and to me, but I cannot take her vibes. I have to run again and feel like a coward.

I have watched Julia all evening long. Her profile reminded me of a cameo cut inset that burned with its distinct outlines into the fabric of my soul. I cried inside and have not advanced a step further. But then, could there be still another time like this? I doubt it. It has already felt like a good-bye to me. Passing at my table she said "I'm leaving at the end of June."

"Blast," I blurted out, "that's in a month's time!" She looked at me with her dusky eyes, a light reflection reminded me of a tear on its high gloss polished shine. How could we make up six months, we spent writing away, and we seemed to think being so close, didn't we? Well, yes is the answer and I won't give-up hope. Book signing is an event for meeting, so nobody will be hurt. Yes, nobody, but she and I.

I've lost her, I thought, her vivid personality, the glow of her eyes that buried me inside and let me swim in the warmth of her tropical lagoon. The slide along her nose to play upon the tips of her finely chiselled lips –

I will become an excited poet, a hard man, if I carry-on like this. I desire her and cannot get closer to embrace her. I wished not to force it, but what if time runs out so fast?

At Kunzelmann's evening we meet again. She is in company and I had missed out on Julia again. For her it's important, it's business and the pleasure of a dinner. For me it's an increased heartbeat and more pain.

"Another time then," I say. She turns, not sure what to say to me. There' only one more book signing event with Phillippa. She is a romance writer for historic novels. I am sure Julia will come, perhaps make some time for me. I have, besides my romantic fantasies with her, collated my love poems, I have written for her, on a CD, I wish to give to her. It expresses my feelings from the first moment I saw her. It's not yet finished with our stealthy relationship, and I cannot wait to slip her my CD and watch her surprised face.

*

My Writing Tools

A different hub awaits us at the airport. We are as usual, too early. This pen, I carry all the time with me, is the one Anetha gave me as a present. It has a steel nib that is bent-up, as if she picked at it in anger, like others do their noses. Pens are like noses, you pick at them, nose them, throw them about, sneeze into them, pick a fight with them, and demolish them. Back again to base. If you feel remorse, you hug them, like a loved one. At peace again with them and inspiration fills the pages through them, as they slide upon the white unruled paper. This one, I am writing recently with, I have inherited after the first one fell down and twisted its nib on impact. I had listened to the first pen's wailing and sorrows for a long time, besides to many stories she had experienced through happenings with her previous owner, Anetha.

I love my new pen. It has a fine nib, usually women prefer, but as it was a present I made use of this lovely lady and wrote much finer and narrower lines with it, useful to fill small notebooks with finer paper. I laud her slick and slender body and stroke her like a lover would stroke his beloved. She purrs like a cat if I do that. There is no pressure necessary to the notebook paper, as it floats like a cloud of blue lines written all over the free pages and follows every whim of my fingertips to write legibly. After I had cleaned it and placed a new cartridge of royal blue ink onto the nib holder, it had been stubborn at first to move. Please don't behave like a hurt teenager. I know you did belong to a great poetess, but I have been on par with her in heart and soul and our minds are comparable, so please get off your high horse and write, ordo I have to lick you? I licked the delicate nib and nothing. I licked it again. At the third time it started to write. Typical woman, I thought, always keen to be licked. I did not say it aloud, in case she took that as an offense. My pen never leaves me abandoned, hangs on me, a truthful mutt. It is always at my side, never runs out of ink, while I write, or suddenly dries out, a wonderful mate full of surprises at times. How would OI not love it?

However, I have a collection of pens and I rotate them most of times, depending on what I write. With Anetha's feminine pen, I prefer to write on the go, and mostly into my small notebooks, I call: journal-poetry. All my pens will have the opportunity to dance upon the silken papers, which I have to choose for their specific performance. Not all papers suit all pens. I have learned through Anetha the science of choosing pen to paper and vice versa. For certain tasks I wake my specific pen from her bed in a specific pouch, where I keep them. There is no jealousy between them, as all – like in a Sultan's Harem – will get a chance to perform. I stroke them and warm them up. I hold them and slowly I feel the connection from my heart and soul to flow from the tip of my pen. Then I know I have the connection to my writing tool. If on top, I happen to be in an artistic groove, my specific pen will be infatuated with me, do its playful dance and perform just fantastically. I can feel it immediately if the story is on good tracks. I love it! All my ink-pens love me, just as much as I love them, even more, as the dropped pen still mourns her retirement, but remained loyal to me. To compensate for her handicap, I use her for some rendering of drawings. That way she is happy, indeed.

I watch a man, looking like a tourist, who watches a black woman waitress in her black tights that sculpt her shapely figure favourably: Taught like a sausage, but aesthetically sensual. The man licks his lips as he takes a sip of his coffee. Immediately Anetha comes to my mind. She loves tight pants and tops showing her figure off. I was always attracted to view the roundness of her body, top and bottom, as I cast my eyes over her. In my mind I stroked her body, as she knew that she created instant desire in me. I thought of all as a fad and did not pay much attention to her dressing-up, just enjoyed all playful moments.

The day I had to travel back and forth to her apartment in town, tired me physically and the endless bus drive drained my energies completely. In my mind though I was awake, vivid and strong, and I yearned for her. She was my potent drug in a continuous erotic tingling that had befallen me like a bug.

I had to catch the early morning bus and therefore to get up at the crack of dawn. I had to reach her that special day, when I could still hug her, but to be in time at her apartment, I had to catch the subway, an hour-long travel by bus later. Well, still loving her as much as I could, I had to help her out with errands, she could not do any longer. In thought I still longed for a moment where we still could embrace our left-over libidos and make love one more time. Was she up for it? Well, I thought, we'll cross that bridge when we get to it, and carried on to reach her place in good time. Strange thoughts recurred and I had to think of bees who loved their queen and then had to die. Had fate reversed matters here with Anetha and me? I had to stop at the post office at Ermou Street and do my post.

When I met Anetha, for the second time, I had lost the first travel-pen she had given me, and I lamented. I had lost it in the bus on my way back to her retreat at the sea, she had offered me and my spouse for a stay. I loved the place with the grand view of the bay with the island shaped like a pyramid. When Anetha listened to the reading of my lines: He had fallen asleep, the pen gliding from his fingers. It fell into the gap between the seat on the bus and its close position to the outer wall. Even a feverish try to retrieve it had failed and it felt to him as if he had lost his last portion of libido he had in store of sharing with her…she stirred. "What's wrong?" She asked and looked at me with concern. "I've lost my beloved travel-pen, you gave me last time."

"Well, it can happen," she said, "wait, let me see." She hurried off. "The one that is a see-through and I use when traveling," I called after her. She came back. "Here is another one. Take mine. I do not need it any longer." She said and placed an identical one into my hand.

The next time I saw Anetha for the last time. Her cousin Athinulla received me, kissing my cheeks. She wrote the beginning to a poem, showing me her pen, Anetha had given her as a present. I saw the third identical pen, Anetha had once collected, and now she shared them with us, her beloved ones, as she called us. She shared with us software and poetry, books she had told me about to read and she valued. Athinulla complained that her pen didn't write properly. "OK," I said "let me clean it for you." I took a paper towel from Anetha's kitchen and started to clean Athinulla's pen. As I returned to the lounge, Anetha wrote a short story. Athinulla scribbled too. "Thank you so much," she said and spoke to me with a warm glow in her eyes. "I will now write a poem, I have not written thirty years ago." She looked beautiful for her age.

"Go for it!" I said. Her eyes fell on my pocket notebook. "Have you written some poems you want to share?" Her eyes beckoned. "Yes, I have. Do you want to hear some?" Anetha stopped writing on her laptop and came closer. "Well, as I have such an eager audience, I will read them out to you."

"But those are private," Anetha intercepted looking at me with a concerned expression. I started to read and the cousins fell silent. Athinulla closed her eyes. When I finished she looked up. "That person must be lucky for whomever the poem was written," she said and watched my facial expression. I would not give away anything, I had promised Anetha, who sighed. I sensed that it would be the last time I saw her alive.

Athinulla wanted to hear more and I sensed that she liked the erotic content of my poems. It stirred her and she gasped. "It's erotic," Anetha blurted out. Athinulla said nothing, her eyes glowed. "It is what I am," I said.

The same day, on my way back with the bus, I wrote a poem for Anetha, who preferred now the company of a younger man, introduced to her by her former girlfriend. My feelings for Anetha were still strong, but I was hurt as 'Her Man', as she had always called me, when she still was in love with me. However, I had acquired an inner strength to deal with such matters of the heart and to convert my emotions into the written words in my note book. I took Anetha's second pen and wrote away. My inner pain subsided as I placed the first words on paper and the story started flowing. Finishing a few pages, my pain was gone, and the bus stopped at the station before I had to get off. I placed the cap on my pen and put it with my notebook into my rucksack. I walked about ten minutes to Anetha's hideaway, where my spouse and I would spend our last night listening to the concert of cicadas. We cleaned her place and packed our belongings. It was time to tuck-in and get up early the next morning.

Damned! Something pricked my chest, as I took my rucksack off entering the tram in Athens. It was a hot August morning and I had an appointment to see somebody from a gallery for a possible exhibition of my work. Then I noticed that the black cap of my of Anetha's pen was missing. I looked for it in my breast pocket of my shirt, but I couldn't find it. Damned! I had lost the cap to the black Parker pen, she had written all her poetry with, and I had continued that tradition. Now, the cap had always been sitting loose, as it had a hairline crack, but despite that I loved the pen. It had been nine years later that I had lost the first pen, Anetha had given to me. Now this one lasted until now and I recalled the many highpoints happening since then.

"How are you?" The familiar voice stirred me.

"OK...Ah it's you, Hana." I kissed her cheeks.

"Let's have some coffee." We took the close-by coffee place, where we enjoyed a cold glass of water immediately. "Have you done your errands?"

"Yes, I have done them in too much of a hurry."

"It's too hot in August," Hana said. "You have to slow down."

"I will, as I have lost the cap of my favourite ink pen," I told Hana about the pen. She commiserated and handed me a blue pen. "It's not ink, but it writes like an ink pen. My spouse used it, he received it as a corporate gift in Japan."

"But I am sure it has sentimental value for you."

"Not to worry, I use it seldom. Just take it." I thanked her, but I asked her if she ever would need it again, to ask it back. She laughed and it felt as if Anna had sent her to look after me, so that I never would run out of ink pens again. I smiled.

*

The Editing Lesson

The morning is not unusual for its pallid light, marred by the sharp rising sounds from a nearby alarm. I am up before the mobile's alarm will sound. That's useless now in any case, and I notice that my head is still swamped by my dreams. Up before an alarm sounds off, calls up psychic powers with subconscious thoughts working in me from the night before. The time, I wanted to be up by, kicks and shouts in me to wake now. Their work fulfilled to their satisfaction, they laugh like public servants, having succeeded to stamp the time indelibly into my mind's consciousness.

In my ritual of cleaning, I rinse off the night's soluble cocoon that kept me cosy and tight below the multi-layered blankets. I am wide awake taking my charcoal moleskin diary to write into, treating it as a journal. I do not mind writing irregular lengths, and at times overflowing into the following days. The diary grid in subdued grey serves as a daily reminding discipline, to put down my thoughts and feelings in prose. If it spreads into an extended inspiration, I use my poetry book with Klimt's *Sunflowers* at present. It has a summer's green overall effect that soothes, with the mustard-yellow suns of the flowers and their brown varying middle fields; decorative, seen from above, as if flying over it. The artistic opposite endeavour to a Vincent van Gogh painting.

It's Tuesday, the thirteenth, a good day for my first lesson in editing text. I enjoy the Write Co.'s classes, especially since I have started. First hesitantly and yet curious, I ventured into a new world, my late friend and poet Anna had started opening-up for me.

I never thought enjoying the extension of knowledge about the basic structures of the English language this much. I needed to learn more about it than a quick brush of general knowledge; Amara told me that as well. This, I thought, is like designing a building. I start an inner dialogue, as always, as I stay as a solitary man in my beloved study, connected by a short walk across the back garden, and a few steps up onto a terrace, from one wooden door to another of our house.

This morning, the thirtieth of June, I realize that some people might be scared by number phobia, stay at home in their beds. Something bad may happen on the thirteenth, I hear people say around me, when I was still small. For me it was always the reverse in a way. It had less significance to anything for me, until Anna related the numbers to signify important milestones, marking events in her short life. I liked uneven numbers and then I began to look at this number phobia in a different light. I was born in my grandparent's house with the number thirteen. Anna added my date of birthday up: "19," she exclaimed, "excellent, reduced that means "one". As you are an Aries, your number relates to the number one Cardinal sign, you see the significance?"

Since then I started adding up figures and reduced them in a kind of mental sport. At times it hit on my inner nerve of caution, especially when Anna died.

I was born on number thirteen, in a village of a defunct K&K Monarchy. The hamlet Felpu, part Austrian, part Hungarian, a mix of controversial cultures and temperaments, was my hometown until I grew-up. When I started asking questions about its history, I received vague or no answers. I started to dislike living on the neighbour's doorstep. People appeared to me strange as I attended to my studies, and I became alienated to the surroundings of my childhood.

I met many peers of my age and we all strived for a Bohemian-style of living. I disliked though the shared quarters in Vienna at one stage of my student life, as I had to book a shared room for myself, if I brought a girl home and needed privacy. Misch, a girl I connected to very well, enticed me to the number's game of reduction by adding up. She bought me a book about the secret numbers of the Kabala.

I could cement my personality to become an individual and stand solitary with ideas and thoughts against the numbers of other peers and architectural students at the Technical University of Vienna. A good place to learn and study, with the city of Vienna as a magnificent background, even if conservative, where new ideas burst forth from us and were immediately refused and ridiculed by the sated bourgeoisie of the ruling middle class.

Here, in Jo'burg, I drive in my ageing Merc, but feel well in it, ageing together gracefully. Time has moulded us into one entity. I noted it all down. The course facilitator pulls me along and I think I have to shed a tear for Anna, who could never attend such a course and workshop, although she longed for one. Now I could see my struggling efforts, an aspiring writer initially, poised with acquiring the tools to advance to a state of an amateur writer.

I am looking forward to grammar lessons. Did I ever? Never had I during my secondary education level, although the teacher at that time tried very hard to insert into us growing rebels, the basic knowledge of the English language.

When I finally arrived in South Africa with my spouse, I realized my poor command of the English language that dated back many years. I had to brush-up my English immediately, in order to survive in the world of my profession, which I mastered. I advanced to top jobs in architectural firms and I enjoyed writing letters and prepare design scheme descriptions within a presentation brochure. Finally, I was able to obtain a project management diploma and communicate with all players in realizing a project from inception, design, and construction documentation to realizing it on a green field. I loved the challenge of leadership, leading by example rather than by theory alone. I believe still that a leader will have to prove himself or herself in deed, not by politics alone, to secure a top position. I was able to bypass politics in favour of professionalism, and to give the client the best product for his specification, in time, and to his budget. Kerzner taught me that in project management. I became one with the aspects of an idea to realize it through planning and coordination into an end product.

At heart, I am an artist though. I conceptualize, I am a draftsman, a painter, a collector of words, a bead-maker from words, assembling chains of jewellery, I'll relate to poetry.

I arrive at the village of office suites, park my car in one of the remaining three visitor's bays. Then I take the sharp right turn uphill to the Curie-rooms. The name symbolizes a strong-willed woman, a scientist, an inventor. X-rays are known to everybody. She brought into this world a great life-saving invention, diagnosis would be impossible without it. I have a chat and banter with Anar, and thus, paying for the course becomes less painful for me.

I have coffee, upstairs, taking my preferred bar stool facing the entrance. Tiff arrives finally. Her faded jeans are her trade mark, threadbare at her right knee. She looks pretty today, less formal without her thick glasses. Then it hits me: she had her eye operation! Great. I call her in my writing Tiff, less respectful, more intimate. She calls herself Tiffany, but when I saw her name for the first time, I addressed her as Melanie, as it came to my mind immediately, and I wouldn't know why. She has shiny long charcoal hair, she keeps today loose falling over her shoulders. Her chocolate brown jersey is tight on her cerise blouse below, she wears over her jeans. She has a prominent silver buckle that suits her jean-style outfit; Levis, I suppose. I respect her, even if I feel more relaxed with her. She has natural charm and a sharp mind. A highly educated woman, she has great editing skills, and she goes for the jugular in a pleasant way. She gives us essence, not waffle. I am glad I am accepted as an elderly person in the midst of a bevy of young and intelligent women, writers, who aspire to become editors, publishers, and event organizers. A mix of youth and experience.

"What do you want to achieve?" Tiff said. "Write it down." We scribble away into our module books, Tiff had handed out beforehand. A plastic pocket with a ballpoint pen and a blue covered examination pad, a slab of Nestle chocolate, a book-marker, and an advertising sheet of the Write Co. neatly stacked inside.

Vari, the cute Indian girl next to me received a red plastic folder. The colour suits her style. I end up with a yellow folder for the second time. The Zulu-woman in a mustard-yellow leather jacket takes the purple one and Somarie, the pale brunette woman takes the blue one from the pile, matching the colour of her eyes.

I observe Vari's profile, fascinating me with the way she talks, curling her full purple lips. She arrived first at the front room this morning. I already sipped coffee. Introducing myself, I took the opportunity of holding her slender hand for a moment and I liked her immediately. At first I couldn't understand her name and I asked her again. For writing's sake, I call her Vari. The class of three women and me, the only man, is definitely a good class.

I have time in between questions and answers to observe Tiff. She's a less depressed person now. Something happened to her. I guess she is in pain at times, and I wonder why she doesn't take any painkillers. I think she does when she leaves for a break, but she will not show the state of her emotional life. Her eyes, now freed from thick layers of glass in front of them, show their colour and beauty. What a difference to last time. Her eyes compliment her long dark hair. She has a southern appearance overlaid with a city elegance.

"Could I open the windows?" she said, and as nobody reacted, I replied "Yes, of course." She leaves us with another exercise. My eyes follow her leaving the room. I hear her chatting to Anar. Her hip jeans look cute on her. She looks young, perhaps 24 or 25, I guess.

We are still scribbling away. Tiff never places us into bad positions, neither feeling suppressed, nor inferior.

Vari and I team-up for some ideas in a brainstorming session. I think she appears to me cuter as time passes and I get to know her a bit. I have another chance of watching her profile, study her fine-boned face and my eyes rest on her beautiful lips.

Tiff tests us for our work. The women, who teamed-up, Lindi and Somarie, are no competition to Vari and me. However, we are most happy when we prove our individualistic styles. It surfaces from a test, writing down associations with a selected list of words, which Tiff hands us. Then as we finished the seven minute working time, she announces "Lunch time."

I did not realize that four hours had passed already, neither feeling famished, nor in need of a break. We fetch our sandwiches and sit outside in the sun. The women discuss general matters. I listen and give my comments at times. Tiff conducts the conversations to maternal matters, realizing that Lindi is pregnant. I see it now, as she has mentioned it, as I sit next to her, observing the gentle swelling of her tummy. Women are conscious of looking good even when pregnant.

I am at Tiff's mercy. Editor women are merciless. However, I hope my writing life will be met by them with fairness. This is what Tiff teaches us, as an editor to become a ghost. I wish Tiff could be my editor and I could afford her. Perhaps I will edit as good I am able to, conscious to support her role as much, as she supports mx work. Then I could be praised as a happy writer.

The course nears its end. We scribble our E-mail addresses for her on a pre-printed sheet. She'll send us some hand-outs on punctuation. I will join her for an advanced editing course as well. I'll book with Anar now. Glad about talking to Tiff and Vari and the other women. If I ever could contribute to Vari's magazine, I'll call her. I will buy a copy to keep me remember about that. Now I can put a face to her name and have its correct spelling. Who knows, I might come up with a story one day, she'd like to feature.

The Guardian Angel

"Where are we? It's rather comfortable here." He sank into a leather chair. Someone served a frothy cappuccino. "Excellent," he said, "I do not need one." He could not detect any signs or advertisements, and voices were hushed and low. How could he hope then to catch a word, as all became muddled and foreign to him?

"I need to know where I am," he said aloud and tapped on the shoulders of a dark-haired woman who paused, throwing glances at him. Yet, she neve3r showed her face and avoided looking at him. Strange, he thought, I might be dead. His hand touching his chest, he convinced himself that he was still alive, except his mind deceived him. All look here tonight as if they are all dead, he mused. Figures appear out of the blue like holograms, a long passage opens up and a centre for learning appears, and a library. He couldn't recognize any of these spaces, although they all looked familiar to him. He patted his face. He seeme3d to be flesh and blood.

What about his contemporaries at this round table? He noticed somebody murmuring to his left, books piled-up high on either side of her pink notepad. "I do know now what to write," she murmured. It'll be a romance novel and rather realistic," she said, handing him a book with a red shotgun shaft. *In Cold Blood* the title read. "But this is not romantic, it's a nightmare, a multiple murder, and you call this romance?" He was upset by the gun doused in blood.

"No, no, no," her voice rattled like pistol shots, "that's not what I said. I write romance, but this is a book I was waiting a long time to read. She smiled like a man who suddenly turned into a woman. Her eyes glowed warm, the only warmth that radiated the softness of a woman. She had big breasts covered with a charcoal striped jacket. Other than that she had no clothes on, sitting in an upright pose on the soft-cushioned chair.

"That's interesting," I replied handing her the book back. She took it and for a moment exposing her large brown

areolas that sat like raised disks on her perfect mammil-
lae, as if delicately carved from mahogany. "I like your
breasts," I said as I gazed at their exceptional beauty.

"Thank you dear," she said in a tone that made us inti-
mate friends at that moment. "Wow," I murmured.

"Have you seen the movie?" she said with her teeth
gleaming in contrasting, sparkling white.

"No," I said, "I don't mind Truman Capote, but I cannot
stand the actor with his squealing voice."

"Hoffmann, you man?"

"Yes, Hoffmann," I repeated after her. "He puts me off
to go and see the movie." Then she faded into the back-
ground as a movie advert. Obscurity reigned. With every
step forward, someone else appeared. One had to be
brave to take the next step.

"Good evening my friend," someone with a distinct ac-
cent approached him.

"Hello," he answered back concentrating for a moment
to recall her name from the last exercise class. "Impossi-
ble, I can't remember," he said aloud.

"Nice seeing you here," she continued. The blond, at-
tractive woman turned her torso and her head from her
seating position. She appeared to be interested in him. It
was unexpected, for he had not given her a more detailed
look-over before. As he stood closer to her, he took the
seat immediately next to her. Her whole body radiated
warmth that enveloped him with a great scent of vanilla
and hibiscus, and she turned him on. His instincts stirred,
but he tried concentrating on social talk. He couldn't think
of having her as a woman before, but he recalled a similar
face of an effeminate man. If that had to be the case, his
transformation into an attractive blond, took his breath
away. He was short of words. Tonight she looked differ-
ent, out of a fashion box. Seductive. Holding his hand, she
introduced him to her husband.

"Hugh," he said and grumbled, as if he had a fight with
her before. He looked dark and looking him over.

"Zsolt," he replied with an undertone, "nice to meet you." He took his outstretched hand. Then Hugh returned to gaze through his book, whose pages he flicked consistently. "He is into figures," the blond woman said with an accent that reminded him of Oz. In his mind Jane of Oz came up, as she talked with an increasing possessive tone in her voice. I'm rather fascinated by her accent, he thought. "Are you writing a book?" She enquired with that slight drawl at the end of nouns and verbs, mastered to perfection. She could turn it higher or lower, he thought. Her knees touched his as she turned in her seat. Then she slithered down exposing her thighs, shedding pieces of her clothing as she twisted and turned. One piece followed another, with every twist of her words she accentuated her denuding act. Her top off, she started to glow, offering him her red lips, as his hands snaked down her neck, along the valley of her breasts, returning to slide back at her sides and then cupping them. She took air in and pushed her body's jewellery out and then sighed, as his palms rubbed across her hardened nipples. "Ahh!" She exclaimed. "Uhh!" She closed her eyes for a moment. "You do this well, I knew it when I first saw you," she gasped. "I'm writing a romantic novel. This is a scene I wished to experience with you, before I started to write." She threw her head back, encouraging him to explore her toned body. He started to slide down on her, as she entered a shorter breathing mode. As he looked up from his kneeling position, he noticed that Hugh had silently disappeared. With his exploring hands on her soft thighs, she opened up to him, she wanted him to eat her. "You are a sexy woman," he whispered, "I do you now." She cried out and he tasted her scent as she started to flow. "Mhh," he mumbled, "champagne and oysters." She laughed. "Let me see you," she gasped, her hands cupped his crotch. Her fingers closed around his bulging penis. "I must go now," he said. "I'm sorry," he frowned. "You should be," she sighed, "you don't know what you'll miss." She said nothing more donning her clothes back in layers. She dressed with quick motions. As he stepped aside, she vanished.

He took a step forward and then back, testing the magical floor. Different faces appeared, like on a huge electronic touch screen embedded in the floor. It made great fun to move whichever way, as one didn't know what to expect next. It became every time a surprise. He rushed forward through an array of faces and bodies. Then a woman appeared in her negligee. "Excuse me," he said, "are you Princess Radzivil?" He flashed a smile. "My name could be *The Wandering Poet*, but some call me 'High There', and others call me 'Sunshine'. My real name is Zsolt," he bowed slightly and kissed the ridge of her hand, as he had learned the noble custom from his mother. "You mean you are related to a Sultan, a king?" She asked and rattled off a series of Turkish rulers from the 16th and 17th centuries. A she called out *Sultan Suleiman,* he gasped. Uhhgg! The one whose bloody torturous acts decimated the Hungarian and Austrian people, as he besieged the city of Vienna from a neighbouring Eastern Hungary under his control.

"Indeed," she said, "you know your history. This is excellent, why don't you write a book?" Her voice rose in excitement, her pale-blue eyes mingled into his, beckoning for his touch. He leaned forward closer towards her and kissed her. It appeared to be the softest kiss he remembered. At that moment she faded. He held a book in his hand she had left him. *The Virgin Lover*, he read on the cover.

As he moved forward, he entered a room with a long table laden with food, smelling deliciously. His stomach rumbled. He left his book on an adjoining table and he moved a few steps back to gain entry. Then he realized that he landed in a seat, he had been sitting in before. The brunette woman with strong teeth and warm-glowing eyes still scribbled feverishly into her pink notebook, her full breasts heaved below her striped charcoal jacket. She looked like out of bed, having slipped on her lover's jacket, her only piece of clothing. Next to her sat a woman with short cropped hair. He approached her.

"Jean d'Arc?" He took her hand to greet her.

"No," she said, "just a look-alike."

"Nice to see you here. I recall you from writing class, we both visited before."

"Yes," she replied, "I recall your piece of a man's twisted soul."

"Do you?" He said astonished. "I vaguely remember it myself. Once my memory used to be better.

"It'll all come back," she said and smiled with a face expressing pain, as if she would need to suffer, or, as if she'd purify herself from an unpleasant past. At that moment he stepped to the side. She appeared crucified on a wooden cross, her body pierced, her skin ripped open from a brutal flagellation: Blood marks all over her delicate white skin, with the gash of a wound below her breast that oozed like a spring of blood.

"Ughh!" He gasped and touched her nailed feet. "You are not dead, are you?" She moved her body.

"I am in excruciating pain – kiss me!" She whispered, "make me come – alive again. I do not – want to die without – feeling – love." He shed his clothes. Her cries for the power of love denuded him. He slid over her.

"Ahh!" She cried-out. "Ahh! You do that just great." Suddenly her hands became free and she stroked his head with feverish and wild movements. Her hands turned into fists pulling his hair in her ecstasy, as he tasted her bittersweet scent mixed with her blood.

He licked his lips. "I am nuts," he said. "My mind is deceived and I am not in a mood to carry this on. The endless game will soon crucify me too. Who will come and love me? Mary Magdalene? Shit! What a dream." He stepped back and forward on this Fata-morgana of his imaginary world. It faded-out soon as all other images and some muffled voices grew louder. Yet he saw nobody. It's like walking in the fog of his mind, he thought, an entirely different world. He turned to find the table laden with delicious food. He stepped into the direction of the smell of curried chicken. After a few tries he found it. Ahh! All sexual images faded in the smell of delicious food. Once they seemed strong and stirring him to the edge of passion's endurance. The pot of desire boiled over and now all of that vanishes in the scent of turmeric and curry spices? "Ah!" He smacked his lips. "What animals we are," he said aloud. In front of him the woman with glowing eyes appeared. She was short and chubby and her jacket reached to the half-height of her bums. She exposed them fully to him, as she bent down to take her food, stretching and bending repeatedly.

"I like your bums," he said and touched them slightly. She turned. "You can do that again later. I am hungry for food now." She said and her breast touched the rim of her plate.

"Mhh," he said, "I am hungry for you right now." His fingers played on her back, sliding down until she screamed.

"Stop it now, or you are dead!" His hand froze between her bums. He could feel her moistness, and he became aroused. A sawn-off shotgun appeared in her left hand. She pressed it into his groin. "I shoot your balls off!" She sounded serious, with a husky voice.

"That would be stupid," he said, "you have better fun with allowing them their natural expression in a playful togetherness, no?" He smiled at her, cocksure, and the shotgun disappeared into her jacket sleeve. She settled down at the table. When he came to sit next to her, she appeared to be in full cry of devouring her food. She ate like a horse, chomping away noisily. She put him off food. He left his plate untouched, offering it to her.

He hurried from the table and stepped onto another square that lit-up in a bright blue light and he stepped into a bathroom. The air smelled of scented salts. When the white cloud of steam parted, he noticed to be in a Turkish bath. "No," he murmured, "not now." The bodies of nude women writhed and slid in clumps of ball-shapes here and there. In the midst of the scene sat Dee-dee, the poetess, reciting a love poem. It must be Rimbaud, he thought, listening to her excellent French – Le fleur du mal – he recognized some lines.

At a clap of hands, all women suddenly donned black and white silken dresses, featuring a chessboard pattern. An emaciated man appeared, pale and lifeless. He moved slowly to the centre of the arabesque tiled floor and looked up with huge, dark, and soulful eyes, citing a poem – Fuck America – Ginsberg wrote this, he thought. All women gasped. The world without love, sad and empty, Goosebumps crawled across his spine. He did not appreciate to be touched by a man. He fled. The poet laughed.

"Afraid of anal?" His laughter carried on as an echo, as he struggled from the maze of passages to break free.

"I like your face," he said. The golden blond angel sat close to him. He gazed at her satin dress that hugged her shapely body. "I am Ron," she said. He frowned. "You mean you forgot the 'a'", he said. Not Rona?" His face relaxed. "No," she said. "I am Ron, your guardian angel." She smiled and he felt a stirring confusion in his body.

"But you look like a woman," he said, shifting from one foot onto the other.

"That may be," the angel said, her clothes fading from the heavenly Michelangelo-body, and she projected a striptease show onto the monitor of his mind.

"This is a great slide-show, "he lauded her. "My god!" he exclaimed as his voice tightened. "You are a well-hung man below and a woman above." She was at first repulsive as a he-she, but the strangeness of having both sexes on one body, attracted him to this angel.

"Do you like me?" Ron said and paraded and turned in front of him. "I am your sweet transvestite," he cooed. He was in a back and forward move, attracted by the woman at the top and repelled by the man below. He could play her as a she and then also as a he. His mind went into a spin of a nightmare. He woke, perspiring and with a fever, his temples pounding. "This is an unusual place for ideas;"

he moaned and turned around in his bed. "It' s too early to rise yet," he moaned in his half-sleep, "I rather go back to my dream.

*

The Lecture

I missed to look at my computer screen for days. It had rained substantially, as a low-pressure system stretched over the city. I did not intend to go down through the long grass, which extended from the main house to my studio, to switch my computer on. What for? There would be messages on the monitor appearing just as well tomorrow. But then, being curious about Elle, or any other Muse, who happened to remember me, this thought took me toward another mood, and I could write a letter perhaps. Just as I set my mind to it, B asked me to take her to her medical doctor.

It's only a twenty-five minute drive in peak traffic time to the northern part of the city, passing the well-positioned suburb of Craighall Park, with street names that supposed to recall their equivalent in London, but perhaps solely by name. Once you have mastered the difficult crossing of Jan Smuts Avenue, then part of the worst traffic obstruction will be behind you. Some people are considerate, like in every city, and others not, subject only to character and not to skin-colour.

One person gives me right of way, while I am trying to get across a car in the last lane, but the man wouldn't stop. He looks at me with a grim expression in his dark shadowy appearance, his middle-finger lifted. I sit still, absorbing the inner explosion. I usually avoid reacting to finger-pointing, but this guy riles me. I am hitting mentally at his attitude and his arrogance of indiscriminate idiocy. It's useless talking to a fool, my inner voice says. This is leading nowhere; maybe the atmospheric low-pressure system has its toll on all of us, probing our patience.

Now the, somebody comes to my rescue, as he hoots at this stubborn bloke to move on. On the roads the brutality has this face of underlying strength of the complex-ridden masses. "L'idiot!" I yell in French. This has nothing to do with racial attitudes, just pure selfish strongman-play to pay me back for sins other contemporaries had committed perhaps, and then he was not even born. So, what has he to offer about human struggles of any kind? It is not written in bright red across my car that I'm from liberal extraction and education, and also happened to be at all times a second-class citizen here!

"Enough!" B said, "and let's rather talk about what we'll need from the pharmacy."

"OK," I reply, "I need Ramace, this bloke just caused my blood-pressure to climb to at least 160." B takes a piece of paper from my notebook, where she jots down our required medicines. I concentrate on my driving omitting the

Scene with the black middle-finger from my mind. I will not drive anymore across this access of Oxford Road again. No. On principle. Now, through the dip into the main road to Sandton. It's much easier and the traffic flow is easing. It's around high noon and the majority of contemporaries are at lunch break. Parking is available and I find a spot immediately. B walks ahead while I check if my car is locked. She's the patient today and I will sit in the doctor's waiting room, on the blue-upholstered chairs, until she' ready.

I take my red notebook from my back pocket, a no-name brand from P'n'P-supermarket. It's good quality for the price, and I prefer to write in ink, a luxury, but I love the sound of the steel-nib's impact on the paper, as it whispers all the words I'll put down. I wonder if somebody else could hear that. It is too noisy though. The hum of the TV with an ongoing cricket match between Australia and South Africa will douse any whispers and even low level conversational talk. The nurses are all in, at times congregating, as if they would prepare themselves with shared confidence for some invisible major tasks ahead. I have seldom seen them assembling around the receptionist's desk. Lee, the tall blond woman from Kwa-Zulu Natal, the thick-set dark haired and short woman, always commenting on one's health, the light-blond Italian woman, who has shown once interest in conversing with me, dialled my number, but when I challenged her, she got cold feet: "I'm much too old for that!" I had to laugh. "It's all in the mind my dear," I replied. She certainly is a sensitive woman and she took me right through to her girlfriend Gia. Bingo! Incredible, they even match in demeanour. I had to think immediately of AyAy and her Greek poet, and then about my mother and her friend, a sophisticated looking Hungarian personality, who was a writer. She always avoided talking about him, even if I asked her repeatedly. She kept his photograph though. Some incidents just pop-out my head. I had to smile, recalling mother who told me in her anger: "You behave just like him!" I thought Mom was stubborn, not anybody else. She had this mercurial characteristic, which I might have inherited.

"B!" The voice of the doc, who calls her by her first name, stirred me from my train of thoughts. It was then that I noticed that I had jotted down some stanzas, and it looked to me a promising start for a new poem. I love these sudden grooves that open up after some hassles along the road driving to the doc's practice, a complete different working habitat.

Finishing the second stanza, B came already back. Her eyes directed to me indicate to join her at the reception desk and pay the bill. OK, I get up. Lee took the account details off her and she is busy punching data into the PC.

"I took last week your money for medication, but it has been paid by your medical aid, it has to be refunded to you." I am confused. She calls the admin-lady for assistance, who just credits my account. Then we move a few steps to the pharmacy at the adjoining room. It's run by two ladies, Deb, a fleshy young woman with rosy cheeks and excellent health, tells me that she is from a blood-donating family. "You have zero? That's excellent! You could save everybody's life," I comment.

"Then we can go to Deb for blood, if we need to," Gia, the pharmacist throws her comment into our conversation, laughing. A woman of sensual qualities, intending to be everybody's friend for those who ask her. Obviously I have been put into the care of her hands, hinting for a rendezvous with 'bella bionda', who took me through to Gia, almost in panic. Deb is prepared for a tete-a-tete, but she is single. I prefer married women as friends, as there are no high expectations then. She finishes her orders, then she smiles and agrees with me on some quirks we seem to have in common, like spending money easily. Leaving with our usual greetings, we proceed towards the grey mass of the colossal Sandton shopping complex. It's a place of noise, hustle and bustle, with a continual rebound of shuffling feet within the movements of masses of people on the polished stone floors.

We found parking at our usual spot, in the second lower basement. The lift takes us up to Mandela Square, we walk to the edge of the Square and through the sunlit open space. The jets of the water features have been arranged in a system, are flush with the surface pavement and are electronically controlled with their patterned functions. It calls in me memories of a similar design at Somerset House, with its more generous arrangement in the open Square, where children enjoyed a game of sneaking through the gaps between the active jet sprays. This one here is a miniature copy of it. We have to snake between a mass of tourists, who photograph their groups in front of the overpowering bronze statue of Mandela. Its size like his philosophical impact symbolizes him to be greater than life, and who does not admire him?

Passed some cafes, restaurants, and shops, observing the crowds, I see that it's two pm by now and the eateries are still filled to capacity. Will we find a place in one of the sandwich bars? At the coffee shop, B fancies, she finds a table at the furthest corner from the coffee machine. The only background noise is shuffling of feet from the commuters between the floors, who move up and down the nearby open stairway. Perhaps I would prefer the atmosphere behind the coffee machine with its plumes of steam, the smell of freshly ground coffee, croissants, and whiffs of cinnamon, now and then, as a recently baked tray is removed from the baking oven.

Finished with our coffees and sandwiches with grilled veggies, we have some talk about remaining chores, and we buy stationary at our favourite shop. We walk back to our car, as I recall that we have to drive to Crawford College later for a lecture and a book-signing event. I've bought a book at X-clusive Books and I try to recall when I was the last time at a book-signing event, since I've left Vienna. I say to B "I think it was the young woman author, who wrote about her experiences as a supplier of snacks for parties."

"OK," she said, without knowing of what I was talking about, "just take care."

I have spent the afternoon reading some chapters of *Gem Squash Tokoloshe* and like Rachel's style. It's easy to read, yet it's already the budding of her own language. She has concocted a story from a photograph that her friend kept about a lost child. A story that she wrote fast, furious, and with passion. I wonder how her face will fits to her way of writing, and her personality. After all, a writer is curious about another writer's looks, besides how he or she writes and expresses her inner world.

There are already numerous cars filling the college's parking lot for visitors. The private school has grown, from the beginning of the pre-school and primary school, to this enormous extent of a college with the best reputation for education. I walk behind other visitors, who seem to walk to the lecture. The staff room is already humming with the voices of assembled people, mostly women, who rule the world of writing to a great extent. I am checked-in for registration. "The buffet is over there," a woman points me to the right, "there's cheese and wine, help yourself." I'll have some white wine, I think and fetch a glass. But the offered wine seems to be too strong for my taste. I get-up and fetch some cheese, goat and Gouda, and a slice of Danish. The wine has gone to my head, unusual, as I have regularly a glass at home with meals and I sip some while I cook a meal.

Rachel is petite and sensuous and she is fitted with a set of antennae every writer will need, to be in tune with his or her inner worlds, being able to get the story down and bring to conclusion. Rachel talks about HIV/AIDS and I have a bit different views with what she reads off her manuscript. Being concerned, as many are, happens to be one matter, but she does not live here and is caught in this consciousness of being a helper and changing the world to become better.

Then the question time starts, mainly about her book, way of research, visiting the places she writes about, and how it all started. One man is stressing the point of experience and fiction, which she answers evasive, but with the conviction of having done enough research enabling her to write about it. I have at times difficulties hearing her soft voice. The man at my right, a few seats from mine, asks a lot of questions. Only one woman asks about publishing. I only absorb the author's good luck of being chosen from one competition, wondering how many she had entered into, before this one that brought her a contract. She has answered all questions and we are told that the next lecture is completely booked-out already. I have not even received an Email about it.

I take my book for signing and tell her my name. "Come again," she said, as it has sounded strange to her. I experience this with English speaking people. While she writes it, I spell the letters to her. "Have you written your book linear?" I ask her. "At the beginning I did," she replies, "and then I was all over the place."

Her signature is intricate, almost a drawing in itself. I only saw her hand moving frantically, almost as if she would cross-out a word that is unsuited for her writing, almost an explosion. I have no time to study it here. There's a queue behind me. I ponder about her characters in the book, I've started reading. She had mentioned the photograph of a girl she received from a friend, who told her the story of an unfortunate child. Rachel affixed the photo-graph to her fridge and it must have grown on her, as she studied it and wanted to know more about the child, whose piercing gaze reminds me of Simon Weil's picture that grows on me. It lies on my writing desk, observing me at work, watching me nod my head to the rhythmic music of Corea, as I type my manuscript into the computer's word-program.

I drive my car into the garage at our home, it's still light and I will prepare a meal for B and myself. I will talk to her about Rachel and read something from her book after supper. After supper I decided to walk to my study, across the terrace, and type a poem: *The Gate.* I have trans-formed it into German: *Die Pforte.* Then, as I finished it, I closed the PC, thinking that perhaps Ina, in Cologne, will like to read it. Maybe Nina will like it as well, if I'll send her a copy to Wiesbaden, to her place of work at the theatre. I feel tired. Time for my bathroom rituals.

I sink into bed, between the pleasant freshness of cot-ton sheets. I sit-up in bed and take Rachel's book. It is reading I enjoy. I'll get the secret of the way she plots her story that captures me. I have exhausted my energy. What did Rachel say? She's writing her second book. It's about an artist – so is mine! Suddenly Crom and Leena, my protagonists come alive.

Fin.

BOOK II

FANTASTIC JOURNEYS

Actress and Artist

He felt that he had slept like a baby. His doorbell rang. He moved from his bed and hurried to the entrance door through his impromptu kitchenette he had designed. It could be his mother, he thought; who else would come at this time in the morning?

As he opened the entrance door, she came into his domain like a breeze of an icy wind.

"Hello sweetheart," she gasped, kissing his cheeks. Her cheeks were cold. "Oh, you are still in bed?"

"Hello Simchi," he kissed her and then rushed back through the short passage to his adjoining main room into his bed. Only then he noticed that he had no pyjamas on. Simchi laughed. "I like your bums," she said teasingly. Then, without much ado, she followed and took her clothes off. "Don't look, please," she pleaded. He wasn't supposed to look at her undressing, but he cheated, and with his right eye, averted from her, he gazed at her. He liked the shape of her pear-shaped bums and her lean back, but Simchi was conscious that he wouldn't see her from the front. Indeed, her best features were her hips and her pussy, besides her beautiful face with dusky expressive eyes. Her breasts were small, like from a child. He liked her despite her lack of fuller breasts. She had a great spirit and a sharp wit, with a healthy portion of cynicism,, if challenged to a mental showdown, as it happened at times with his friend, he called Henri - French for Henry - as his face and stature resembled Toulouse-Lautrec. Simchi was critical and she had an analytical mind that could irritate his own personality, being all gut-feel and opposite to her bluestocking outlook on life.

They cuddled and he warmed her up. She asked him to make love to her in missionary style, where she could feel his movements best. Circling his waist with her legs, clasping him tightly with a great expression of lust, her lips opened and she gasped. She is wonderful, he thought and became lost in her, digging into her soul.

The party was on the go, but his friend, Henri, phoned him rather late to join in. Besides studying for an exam, he needed some distraction, and his mind was spinning. He could though ill afford to stay out late, or indulge into consuming alcohol. His friend's rented condominium at this time of his final year of studying in Vienna, was indeed spacious, it had three rooms. Lucky for him, it was close-by, a mere half hour walk from his study. There were a few girls present. One blond woman who caught his eye, was busy kissing someone. She looked at him as he passed and she gasped as he pinched her bottom

Henri received him with a hug and introduced him to the people around. He asked Henri about the blond girl. "Oh, that's Carol, she is sweet, known as the virgin-groupie." He looked at Henri astounded. "She stays with you, if you ask her, but you cannot screw her with a full penetration," Henri chuckled. He was fully attentive to Henri's words, who continued "you may touch her though and do what you like, without the final act; she's still a virgin."

"OK," he said, "thanks Henri and settled down with a drink. Later she came to him, as he listened to music in Henri's study. She said hello and he rose to dance with her. Her sensuality had a magnetic effect on him and she looked pretty. They kissed. She loved kissing, being darned good at it. "You'll stay?"

"No," she said, "I want to go, perhaps stay at my girl-friend's place."

"Where is that? He asked.

"Oh, close-by, towards upper town." She smiled at him.

"OK," he said, "I'll take you there." She agreed. He had noticed that the address she had given him was not that far from his studio either, but he said nothing. They said their farewells to the remaining guests, who all were in high spirits and Henri joked about his work to be cut-out.

They left the party in a good mood, a new loving mood and two equal awakening hearts in love. He recalled the words of his elusive girlfriend, Simchi, who loved him, perhaps never taking him seriously and then left him for the next eligible man available. She always had to compensate for a lack of beautiful breasts, and at times she teased him about the size of his penis. Well, he always thought about himself to be normal and never had problems with erections. He was medium through and through and he was always rock-hard. Why did she come to him then, if he was not satisfactory to her taste? He stirred from his thoughts as he felt Carol taking his hand.

Carol was singing and she had her final year at an acting academy. She had a master class appointment in two days, on Monday. When they passed the inner city, relaxing between kissing and petting in the romantic 'Burggarten', they crossed over the Square to the former 'Emperor-Palace', then passed the 'Theseustempel towards the Parliament building. He told her about the architecture and the architects involved in these buildings, about the influence of Greek Classical art that had inspired Viennese buildings in the era of the Classicistic style. She loved as much listening to him explaining building styles and art, as he loved listening to her recitals of poetry and observing her short acting stints she had to practice. If he studied at one of the best architectural schools in Vienna, so did she study at one of the best acting schools in Vienna, and their educational institutions had both the highest standing in their respective fields of science and the performing arts.

Her girlfriend was not at home and Carol was disappointed. "Never mind," he said, "you can stay over at my place."

"But…I am – " She sounded alarmed.

"That's OK," he cut her off, as she hesitated to finish her sentence, prepared to speak about her attitude to sex before marriage. "I respect you, Carol, don't worry, I'm not a beast."

"OK," she said with a smile. "I like you." They crossed the 'Burggasse' and the city's railway line and in the next street, at a corner building, his study was located. He unlocked the front door and walked ahead a passage to his place. Unlocking the glazed door, he let her enter.

She liked his pad, an artist's atelier and a cosy place for a tete-a-tete. She could roam about the two rooms and act out her assignments. He undressed and watched her soulful act, then tucked below the covers. She went to the next room with the kitchenette and a washing facility, a dining nook, and a wardrobe, took her clothes off and joined him in bed.

She was warm and pleasant, cuddling like a rabbit, arousing him. "Be careful," she said, "I'm still a virgin and wish to keep that for my future husband."

"Yes," he said, "I will be." He played with her vulva and she became wet. He was sliding only his crown against her clitoris, and he could feel her intact hymen. She kissed him and then he kissed her nipples. She liked that. Then he played his rubbing game until he came, placing his penis onto her belly. He took a towel from the chair next to his bed and cleaned her off. She turned around, being at ease, relaxed that he acted as he had promised her. Close together they fell asleep.

In the morning she stirred first playing with his erection. Then, as he woke and got up, she wanted him to caress her, offering her breasts to him. They took turns to wash watching each other and taking delight in the youth and beauty of their bodies. Then Carol made coffee and afterwards they went for a morning stroll. She was in high spirits and she played for him a scene from Romeo and Juliet, followed by another sketch. This went on for some time and he had to go back and study for his exam the next day. He accompanied her to the subway station nearby, below the bridge and she said good bye, kissing him gently. "All the best for your exam," she said.

"And also for yours too!" he replied and kissed her cheeks. She disappeared in the last coach of the subway. He would see the cops of blond hair fading away as she waved at him, before the train was swallowed by the void of the tunnel.

Simchi wanted to be taken to bed by him for some time now, as she had chosen him to be the first one who took her. She wanted to be deflowered by him.

"Take me tonight, Joey."

"OK," he said, trying to be calm and cool, but his heart was beating loud in his ears. He had his work cut-out with her. It was one thing to be aroused and it was no problem for him, and he kept hard for some time. She took her clothes off and he was not supposed watching her. >Suddenly she came to bed and stretched out under him. He was keen to give her all he's got, but then recalled his friend's advice: Be gentle at first. Once he had penetrated her, she seemed to have pain and slowly he massaged her pain away. She looked cheerful and she encouraged him. He could see that she felt well. The first time he came quicker than she did, but then hard the second time, she was already responding to his thrusts, and pulling him closer she pressed against him. He had no difficulties to be aroused a third time, as he enjoyed her gasps and cries, and she had turned-out to be insatiable. It was all great fun for him, and he did not know how deeply this first fuck affected her. She loved him in her own way and to her own set of rules she had established for herself: Free Love. He didn't mind. She had finished acting school in town and she had been immediately engaged for a play in a nearby town outside Vienna, famous for its summer festival. He observed the papers. She got good reviews. He had no time to see the play, as he had to work hard during his final year of studying, writing the 'Second State Exam' before the summer break. Finally, the verbal exam for obtaining his architectural diploma in September, caused less pressure exerted on him, as he could prepare for it at leisure during his summer vacation.

Simchi came frequently to his pad, whenever she felt a longing and was sure about safe sex due to her arithmetic,

56

counting the days since her menstruation. Then, it was the only birth-control method that allowed them to enjoy proper sex and the only one available to her. Afternoons were her favourite time and to her it was adventure, excitement during the pause of performance at the theatre, and a refreshment of her spirits. For him, it was receiving a compliment of being perhaps embedded in her always as her first man, and a pleasant break from the slogging of his studies.

She was direct: Kissing, undressing, and slipping into his bed, while he stayed outside the room and once ready, she'd call him to join her. She stretched out supine and he would arrange himself over her. Once settled on her body, she'd circle his waist and enticed him to perform with love-making, which she enjoyed only this way. He was given some advantage over other men in her life, she said to him smiling mischievously. Once she had climaxed, she slipped to the side and as they relaxed, side by side, she told him about this man who had proposed to her. He sensed that she had found somebody, who could look after her financially as well. Her pedantic mother had agreed to her choice. "You must take that chance." He could not afford to think about marriage, besides, he did not particularly believe in it. Yet, he didn't say that to her bluntly, but he was saddened that he would lose her so soon.

"It hurts," she told him.

"Yes, it does," he replied. "Love always hurts. See what I paint?"

"Yes," she said, looking at his collection of abstract paintings stacked against the wall, besides his favourites, he had hung. He would show her all he had done lately on impulse, hopping out of the warm bed, lighting a cigarette and holding the paintings in front of his naked body. She sighed. Then she dressed again and left. He felt empty for a while. Then he slumped into bed and slept, not sure if the expression and intensity he put into his paintings, was not greater than making love to her.

He slept until Beryl came to see him. She wanted to sleep with him for days, but he had refused to make love to her on grounds of disliking a coitus interruptus, she subjected him to. Beryl did not trust the counting method Simchi adhered to, but then he couldn't stand to fuck her and jump-off at the last possible moment before he ejaculated.

"Use a condom then," Beryl said.

"I hate these insensitive late rubbers," he concluded. He liked the way she wanted sex with him and soon, using the counting method and forgetting the interruptive method, they made love like two fiery animals, spiced-up with their fitting bodies, matching well, yet never sated in their wildness. They were protesting lovers, protesting against a hypocritical society, and the strict archaic rules of religiously obsessed people, scoffing at them openly.

They made love everywhere they could think of and had an impulse to do it: In an old-fashioned telephone boot, with small windows; and in the car, parked underneath some trees, near a church. Once he could take her to a choral concert and then, as most seats were taken, she sat in his lap behind the organ. There in a corner he seduced her and she straddled him. It was their most exciting time. He recalled their union on a park-bench, and during a walk into the woods, in the elevator that didn't work, and during a tobogganing midnight. There were opportunities they never missed, but her aunt spied behind them. Yet they managed to be together as lovers, even under her watchful eyes, as soon as she fell asleep. They had paradise on earth and by now he had mastered birth-control with his technique he had put himself together, also knowing her intimately, helping his timing. Her sister had been sent out by her mother to check on her and call a halt to her attitude of free love and seemingly indiscriminate copulation. She wanted him to be her man and he was. Finally, her mother put pressure on him to form a more legitimate bond with her and they became engaged. However, something fundamental, like the former magic of their lovemaking had been lost .It was the absence of an immediate excitement of adventure, the protest, the motor that was inducing great sex in them. He felt caught as a bird locked in a cage, desiring freedom, also in sex.

Lilian was a passionate woman, an excellent actress, and she wished to seduce him at a party. He was into her, their chemistry was right. Sensing her arousal, whenever they touched hands, he finally kissed her and asked her to come with him to the balcony outside the flat, where the party was into full swing by now. She was horny, but she would not drop her pants, clasping him and rubbing herself madly on his erection. He gave up on her, his lips bruised from kissing, but she became aroused again touching his hard erection, simulating a fuck, wanting him. His hands posed to take her pants down. "It's only for once," he whispered.

"I'm getting engaged tomorrow," she replied.

"OK," he said, "I like your passionate body moves and your sexual readiness, your wild simulated take me-in." She wouldn't stop grinding her pussy on his hard-on, eager to get him to come, but to her surprise he didn't. She stopped suddenly and left him hurrying to the bathroom.

He had worked in Africa for fifteen years, when he met a client, who wanted him to build his headquarters. The work was magnificent and the whole scene was set for him to become a prominent architect. One day, John, the director of the company, approached him: "Stella, the daughter of his counterpart at the German headquarters, would like to come to Africa and finish her practice year to be enriched by this experience in a foreign country. Could he take her under his wings?"

"Yes," he said. Stella appeared the following month, a pale and delicate young woman, with lively grey eyes and fine lips, happy like a lark. He took her out a few times and she left like a good friend. She had extended her stay and travelled to Cape Town. She sent him pictures from her holidays and the ones she had asked to be taken from them together. She ventured about the Cape Province and enjoyed traveling the dusky lands.

Time passed. He had successfully finished his acknowledgement of being a professional architect in South Africa on his own. He had a harder working life, but he was happy. Politics, like weather patterns change and he found life becoming unbearably hard, high and dry for work. One day he turned to writing. Soon he had read current books and he reviewed them for a reading club. Further, he practised and practised his daily writing. Working at his discipline, he became, he became prolific and established a reputation among his friends and lovers.

One day he came across her address on the Internet and he wrote her a letter. She responded. "Look at her," he almost yelled, "Stella had become an actress! Indeed!" She performed at the theatre and the names of theatres and cities she wrote down where she performed, were all foreign to him, but one did strike a note: Wiesbaden. Out of the ringing of the word appeared the face of Simchi, who had been telling him about the place, where she would have liked to perform. Such are coincidences! Stella pictured on the program leaflet, a pretty, young, and self-assured woman with such great talent. Bravely and with great courage, she had changed her plans in choosing a difficult profession. Good girl! He praised her. She had many engagements, her contracts were extended and she was in business. She had sent him a photograph with her parents and her boyfriend. He still liked her. Their correspondence had started many years hence, now it had found a resonant echo. He was in the mood to write her and she was spirited enough to respond. He always sensed in her this free spirit and he hoped she would stay a Muse now, even if she was involved seriously with her boyfriend.

Would she marry? He did not mind, he knew she had a mind of her own and she would carry-on writing to him. Her last photograph showed her in a pensive mood. She was loveable. Her wishes for a good new year were heart-felt, she had written in her handwriting with silver ink. He would respond with some pictures he composed on his PC and create an interesting card, or letter, something individually enticing. He'll send her some poems and also a story about the Cretan city of Chania, he had written during his trip there. See what she says. He was delighted with her, close to falling around her, hissing her and then, who knows? Between an actress and artist the smallest tip of the intuitive scales could create a spark of inspiration. And then there's hardly a holding back as their horses of fantasy will gallop across the canvas he is painting of her.

*

Alta's Abduction

He wakes at the end of a tiresome night. "Not enough sleep," he moans and gets up to seek relief in the adjoining bathroom. Physically he feels better, but his teeth ache, as if some fever had seeped into his lower gums and he is bound to become a victim of his dental surgeon again. But he had just visited the dentist. He must sleep more, take a painkiller and soothe his neuralgic uproar that had lodged itself since a few days below and between his teeth. They felt being pulled in a sensation of an urge to bite upon something chewy that would lower the tension. He felt tense with a longing for more sleep. "Ah, some sleep! Relief, relief!

What a strange place this had now become! He used to drive to this underground parking for the last years and it was darn easy. Not any longer. The small, blue car in front of him is stranded right in the centre of the drive. Its emergency indicators blinking. He drives around it carefully, as a black face in blue worker's gear and crash helmet signals him a deviation. He has to reverse and then take the road to the left. The petite lady with the hollow cheeks and bony fingers is still concerned to signal her distress to the banked-up cars behind. Why did nobody bother to place a no-entry sign before the garage's access road? He couldn't understand. Probably he must have missed that, but then all cars behind have missed that too. He recalls dark faces and relates it to Africa. But which city is this? He has opened the window at his side and he felt the warm air, but it was dry. "It can't be the coast near Durban then, besides he would have recognized the city. He recalls the past drives there, an uphill road passed the complex of Westgate's imposing stretch of shopping halls and the colonnaded palm trees. He observed the new style architecture, sleek and shiny metallic, reminding him of boats and sails. At that point he would again drive downhill and then suddenly have a great view of the Indian

Ocean's blue and endless stretch across the horizon, the city opening up at a greater distance to his right.

He drove around the streets and lost his way. He'll rather park his car here, where he still noticed clean streets and enough parking space available. He couldn't see the parking sign for the deviation to lead him to the garage of the newly built centre. Now he remembered that he had an appointment to see the dentist, who had changed his address, but there were no streets names visible. He parked his car at the kerb and locked it by pressing the centre part of the key. The key wasn't his usual key, the plastic tag attached was worn and the writings were illegible. He wished to place the key into the second front pocket of his moon bag, as he always would do it, but he had none placed around his waist. He pocketed the key and walked across the newly-surfaced street to enter a shop selling spices. The scent of sweet and peppery fragrances was pleasantly stimulating. "Like at the North coast," he said to himself aloud and a well-shaped woman with a face that blended with the cocoa-colours, smiled at him and wished him a good morning.

"Can I help you?" she had a magnetic presence.

"Yes. Could you tell me where I am? I've lost my way." She said something in a strange language, he couldn't understand at all. Finally he shook his head and lifted his shoulders in despair. He looked at her. She had long, sleek fingers with which she pointed at his heart, whereby falling into bouts of laughter. She took his hand and pulled him through a curtain with colourful glass-beads, struck by a powerful light, spreading dancing specks of changing patterns onto the opposite dark-red-painted wall.

When his eyes adjusted to the dim inner atmosphere of the first room, he could see a bevy of beautiful girls assembled in one room, attending to a game and giggling. Some were loosely dressed and bare foot, others were naked to the waist, moving their nubile bodies back and forth. "Where are we?" he asked. The woman at his side smiled. His first thought was: An oriental pleasure palace.

The dusky-eyed woman who accompanied him to a room nearby, started to undress him. Then she prepared a bath and continued to soap him and then wash him thoroughly. She dried him off and then she brought him a white cotton caftan with blue embroidery. Then she oiled his body and treated him with a massage. She always giggled when she saw his stirrings and when his body reacted to her touches. At one stage her sensual touches aroused him. Then she smiled making approving noises. He felt fine. Suddenly he saw a bed with immaculate white linen and an embroidery of erotic scenes on the cushions. It reminded him of Indian motives from the Kamasutra he had a liking for. She had put-on soft oriental music that reminded him of Chatur Lal, recognizing the sitar and tablas.

The sweet and spicy scent of incense lay heavily on him and he spun into a realm of dizziness leading him to a world of sweet erotic pictures. The dusky eyed woman from the shop, who tended before to his cleanliness, massaged his head and neck, while another, younger woman stroked his feet. He relaxed, with all thoughts of his whereabouts fallen by now to the wayside, swept away more and more by the sensual stroking of their fine and slender fingers. The younger woman's fine blue-green dress slipping-off at her left side, exposed her beautiful areola and her small but firm nipple, he desired to kiss. He began feeling high, walking on air, in midst of a paradisiacal garden, in a tropical warmth that denuded the shrubs and trees of their leaves and strange erotic symbols grew on them everywhere. A beautiful girl beckoned him to bath with her in the iridescent turquoise waters of a fountain. She jumped on him several times, but she failed. Her top was perfect and Venus-like; her lower part below her navel was the body of a fish. Then a strange thing happened, after she poured him a drink from the top spout of the fountain. He grew immediately a fish body to match hers. She kissed him with an inert fire and then copulated with him like fish do. Humans and fish with human emotions in kisses and slippery feelings as fish in contrast.

He gasped, the women had taken turns to devour him and he was burning in a fire that spread along his abdomen to his chest and his neck and to his face, and it gave him a short breath. He woke. They both were naked at either side of him, smiling, teasing him, giggling and kissing him. He felt pampered, warm and refreshed. He got-up and had a good look at them before he intended to leave. Then, on the spur of an erotic spark, he decided to go back to bed. He was on fire and he wanted to take the young and lithe lass. This game went on and on. He had lost all sense of time. In the morning as he woke to some noises, they were gone. His clothes hung neatly on a hangar, cleaned, and his soft top felt washed and his shoes had a shine. He dressed.

His cellular phone rang. "We have a meeting at ten. Are you all right Joe?" It was Gord.

"Thanks god you are calling me," he retorted in a hoarse voice. "Yes, yes," he stammered. "Tell me Gord, could you fetch me? I had a bad night."

"OK, sure," Gord replied, "at your house?"

"NO, no," he said hastily, "I'm not at home."

"Oh, you loafer you," Gord pushing out his raucous laugh. "Wait!" He shouted, opening the door, exiting the room looking for someone. Nobody was around. There, at the end of the room with the glass bead-curtain a charwoman was busy. She couldn't talk. The environment had changed. The walls were all white; he was irritated by now again. "Gord? This is a strange place. I'll have to call you back soon, OK?"

"Are you all right?" Gord sounded concerned.

"Yes, yes, I just have some amnesia, but I'll search for the address." He ended the talk and headed for the entrance door. The shop was there, spices and all. He could smell the scented air before he entered the shop through a curtain of glass pearls. A wiry brown man appeared in khaki clothes attending to a set of ledgers. He looked up: "Can I help you?" He was relieved, at last he could now communicate and find answers to his many questions.

"You will find this strange, but where are we?" The brown man looked at him sharply with intelligent eyes. "We are in Vib's Spice Emporium. I am Raj, her brother."

"Pleased to meet you, I am Joe. What city are we in?"

"This is the City of Stars, little Delhi, you could say. A stone throw away from the City of the Sun and Moon."

"Aha," Joe said, "the Casino and Gaming Empire."

"Well yes, all the people from the continent come here on a special deal to play. Yesterday was their night and we had an Indian-theme party. Did you enjoy it?"

"Yes," Joe said. He noticed the photograph of a young woman with soulful eyes, being prepared for marriage, with all the henna-painted beautifications. "My daughter," Raj said.

"She's pretty," Joe said taking the photograph from the table.

"Yes," Raj agreed and sounded sad. "She is no longer with us. She passed away last month. The pain of her loss is still with me."

"I'm sorry," Joe said, "my condolences. I - , I thought to recognize her from last night's party."

"No, no," he said quietly, "that was her sister Alta." Joe kept silent. It was the girl he had desired and went back to bed for all night. She was wonderful, with bursts of passion, as far as he was able to recall.

"Raj, do you mind giving me her mobile phone number?" Joe looked at Raj who looked for a piece of paper.

"No, no," Raj said quietly, busying himself to write down Alta's telephone number, mumbling aloud as he scribbled.

"Good morning Joey," a radiant, dark-haired woman with a deep olive complexion entered the shop. "How are you love?" She cooed and as she was close enough, she hugged him, kissing his cheeks. "You look well. Have you been looked after?"

"I am well."

"Have you met my brother? All's well now." She was overflowing with a motherly kindness. "Sit here, I'll fix you coffee, you look like you'll need some." He went into the adjoining room to her desk that seemed to be her office. He sat down in the chair he recognized. Then slowly all came to an orderly place in his mind. With all these last day's events cascading in his head like in turmoil, he had found his Indian lady friend, almost an impossibility, yet reality. She came back, smiling and with a scent of sweet citrus fruit airing her luxuriant appearance. "But Vib, I – this is "–

"Take this," she cut his stammering and handed him a pill. He took it and she disappeared again, reappearing shortly with his coffee. He placed his nose to it: "Cinnamon, mhh, excellent, you remembered Vib, how I like to take my coffee." He sipped it and let it cool down enough not to burn his lips on the edge of the cup. He knew this cup; it was dark-blue, decorated with a scene from Classical Greek mythology. He felt better.

"I wanted to tell you about…"

"How is life Joey? Tell me, how did you know that you'll meet me here?"

"Well …" he cannot seem to get a chain of thought into a sequence yet. "I wish to talk to you alone, Vib."

"Let's go then," she takes his empty cup, "I'll be back in a minute." She has a few words with Raj and they exchange some business matters, while he waits for her behind a shelf with goods, studying her figure, holding a small packet of Oregano in his hand, feeling the substance of his favourite spice between his fingers. He thinks of Cynthia, the woman who came like a spook into his life. She had many names related to Artemis and she had taken on many shapes of different women since. The face of Alta appeared in front of him as Vib came to take him to a nearby speakeasy. He said good-bye to Raj and Vib exited the shop with him, stepped into a narrow road outside, which turned in a bend to the left.

Vib took his hand and she hurried to a small tavern at the end of the street that opened up to a small Square. *Idira,* the curved letters said, painted by an artist, showing a sleek jug from which water was pouring.

"This is a place I know," Vib spoke elated and with some excitement. She took a place in the corner of the tavern, divided from the main room with some plants.

"Vib, I am confused," he started immediately. Vib waved her arm at the waiter and ordered a jug of wine and some antipasti. He poured his story forth. This time she let him speak without interrupting him.

"Now then," he concluded, "I am lost, cast-out, thrown into a cold night and to the wolves."

"No," she replied, "you were thrown to warmth and into a paradisiacal place last night, finding pleasure. You were thrown to the threshold of my soul. I love to have you."

"You say that beautifully, Vib, lyrical like a poet. What was his name?"

"Zelan," she said.

"I was thinking of the Indian poet Rabin…" he struggled to remember.

"Oh you mean Rabinhadrath Tagore," she completed the name.

"Yes," he said, "that's the one!" They exchanged some common interests that had brought them together in the past. She recalled the time when they had met on the Internet chat program and they became friends. He let her talk now and she poured her emotions onto him like the icon on the tavern showed the overflow of water: Life, he thought.

Vib glowed, her olive skin became a shade lighter, translucent and velvet-like to his touch. She took his right hand and placed it on her generous bosom. "Do I love you! I am glad you came." He felt well in the secure folds of this earth-mother with a golden heart that showed upon her face. Her skin turning a velvety-cinnamon, and as she turned he touched her long braided hair, let it slide through his slightly closed palm of his hand. It caused a warm sensation in him, starting in his loins, just as he ended at her lower back, surprising him.

"I love your hair, Vib, and I cannot get enough of stroking it, while I gaze into the mystical ebony of your shiny eyes." She kissed him with small kisses to his lips. Her lips felt full and sweet, the taste of cinnamon lingered on his tongue tip. He looked deeper into her eyes that glowed in a fire setting his libido alight.

"Let's go," she said, "and rest. After that we'll tend to all your matters. As she rose, bending forward, he could see into the generous soft folds of her cleavage and he stirred feeling dryness in his mouth. As he licked his lips reaching for a sip of water, she smiled her mysterious smile: In her eyes were reflections of lush green and dark coloured amber bodies falling in succession. He thought of her in the nude, stretched-out on a light-blue and green linen covered bed.

"What are you thinking Joey?" She took his hand and exited with him her favourite tavern through the back door, then up a flight of steps, across an open passage and finally a steep ascending stair. She went ahead, while he climbed behind her, edging closer to watch her thighs moving, as she had lifted the hem of her dress. He could see that she had no panties on. He reached for her thighs touching them gently. Surprised by his sliding touch, she omitted a slight shriek.

On top of the stairs she paused, being out of breath. "Joey?" He came close to her and as they breathed into each other, he pressed himself onto her, kissing, clasping, and seeking to stoke this sudden fire she had set alight, already in the tavern with her eyes and the wine, her scent of exotic spices, following with touches and kisses. Now he craved for her body, luxuriant and powerful, a mountain of desires he wished to climb immediately.

She opened the door and his fingers at her back were already opening the buttons of her dress, sliding her silken dress from her left shoulder and then the other one. She stood mesmerized as he clasped her huge breasts from behind at first, then turning her around he kissed her deep and fell over her sinking to his knees. He got intoxicated on her velvet skin and the folds as they moved towards the wide bed. She fell upon it and stretched out wide as his welcome weight pounded on her.

"We thought you'll never make it today," Gord greeted him, fetching him from the *Tavern of Heavenly Delights,* where he had phoned him from. The young girl selling roses in the adjoining shop, spoke enough English and she helped him trying to establish all identifications necessary for his orientation and existence, he was still doubtful about. Place, city, street, country, she repeated, as she wrote all data onto a sheet of paper, she uses to wrap roses into. Joey asked for two dozen roses, she would select for him to be delivered to the spice shop in *Vib's Spice Emporium,* "Yes," she said, "she knew it, as it was not far from her shop: The adjoining Square with the fountain.

He couldn't recall the fountain, but was relieved she knew the shop. Gord phoned him on the landline. He was careful with telling him about his bad accident. At first there was nothing visible on him that would indicate serious injuries, except for some cuts and bruises that were immediately taken care of. A young lady doctor on duty at the local private hospital gave him an injection to counter the effects of shock. After the necessary tests she found that he could leave, but not drive a car yet, and to take care. She asked him to return in a few days for all results. He felt fine. He even hired a car the insurance company paid for. Then as he got lost eventually, he had a lapse of memory.

"Your car was towed to the panel beaters, your usual workshop had agreed to. It is bad, but not a write-off. There's lots of damage to the body. I'll tell you details later, for now I am glad you are well." Gord concluded his talk, "I'm on my way to fetch you."

"OK," he said, "I'm glad you are coming, Gord."

Slowly the missing pieces of the mosaic to the complete picture started to fill the gaps and complete the map of happenings in his mind. The crashing of the Four-by-Four into him, his reflexes taking over at an instant, rolling, tumbling; fortunately he could avoid a frontal, disastrous hit. His waking from an alp, voices of the men lifting him, the siren of an ambulance, and his feeling of nausea. The siren of an advancing police car and the screeching of the mobile bed toward the emergency unit at the hospital. He recalls the close blue eyes of the lady doctor examining him. Then, slowly he came to himself and he wanted to go. The lady doc was young, an intern, just having finished medical school. She took her task pedantically serious to the book, and she told him that respectively. He relaxed, she was sweet and professional and he neither wished to interrupt her, nor to disrupt her medical routine she was trained-in. She was serious, but smiled as she found out that he could leave. He couldn't recall any close relative besides his spouse, he didn't want to worry, but solely his friend Gord.

"That's fine," the doc told him, "and you are indeed considerate!" He bought a health bar and coffee at the canteen and brought for the lady doc, who had a long shift today. She thanked him. He took her hand and it felt slightly cool with her long fingers in his palm. A healer's fingers, he thought. She smiled at him, lithe, elphin-like, and delicate but toughened-up, an Angel-Amazon, he told her. Now she laughed. He would like to be back to take her out on her free day. He jotted down her cell-phone number. "Rather leave me a message," she said, "You know how busy we get here."

The compact Citroen was delivered to him. He could see the driver arriving through the windows of the canteen, where he had waited. He enjoyed driving it with ease. It had a navigational system and he tried it out immediately. No way will he lose his way again. He recalled that Gord had mentioned to him meeting about another job in two days, they usually were called upon together. This time it was a rather extensive refurbishment of the entertainment centre of the *City of Stars*. That's when he got lost and nobody knew where he was. He had not turned-up at the hotel Gord's secretary had booked.

Gord turned-up in his sleek silver arrow. He recalled the compact modern black Citroen, Joe had driven from the hospital to here. "There's Gord," he said to the lass tending to the bouquet of roses.

"Hello Joe," Gord was flashing his teeth as he greeted him, then seeing the pretty girl with the roses. "I ordered some," he said to Gord, "for a woman I met, who is from the poet's club."

"I'll order some too," Gord said and chose a dozen for delivery to the Star's Hotel. He paid and left. "Young Joe, how's it?"

"There's it," Joe said, "stop." It was his black Citroen.

"Leave it here," Gord said, "we'll come back again." Joe noted the number on his registration plates down: GHX 121GP. Indeed, he noted that this were not his usual number plates from home. Though it was about a three hour drive at easy speed. He sighed and mumbled.

"Don't worry," Gord said, "we'll fix you up." After some turns and bends, Gord drove his silver arrow down the final straight road as if it would fly along an invisible path like an arrow, indeed, flaming in the sun and aiming at the heart of the entertainment Eldorado in Africa of the South. The low voltage stars had descended above the entrance and Gord rode-up Milky Way. In the centre of the he knoll that extended like a giant knot was Andromeda, the galaxy with her billion stars, a magnificent dome of plasma and light that changed the light images on its translucent skin with a program that changed itself. Light-plays reflecting the play of pleasure with super imposed projections of art and photographs that melted into an aesthetic overkill.

The meeting went ahead, the presentation he had to talk to was all taped and with a slide-show of the latest computerized quality that was impressive. Even Gord was taken-in by Joe's professional aptitude and his fusion of artistic and technical proposals. There were two major variations that had to be voted on, and as Gord explained to the projections related to time, type of construction, and costs. Then after a break for a light lunch, the decision had to be announced. They had won the contract ahead of another competitor was the good news, but the cherry on top meant that the Client panel went for the top notch refurbishment, the most expensive. Gord was ecstatic. He invited the Client body for a Roman party, he intended to arrange at the signing of the contract. Then he urged Joe to accompany him to the Roman style Caracalla Hotel, where he had reserved rooms and the luxury of a Roman bath ritual for them.

The rooms were magnificent with mosaics of great beauty. It reminded Joe of Pompeii, the walls decorated with similar frescoes in fine muted colouring. Gord had reserved him the Ovid-Suite. He loved to know him in midst the erotic scenery he knew Joe appreciated. Joe smiled, it was a poet's dream, his heaven on earth. Indeed! He was impressed. Joe wished to fetch Gord and to see his suite. It was divided into two sections, like his. The entrance and the lounge was decorated with wall paintings featuring Caesar and Augustus and their times. His luxurious bedroom with a gilded bed showed scenes from the *Decameron*. "Truly magnificent, Gord," he lauded his choice of suites.

"Let's get pampered a bit," he smiled showing his strong white teeth, laughing a jackal's laughter, Joe had only heard once before, whenever he was highly excited. "The two sisters are already waiting for us." Gord glowed

"A bacchanal?" Joe wanted to know, but Gord just laughed aloud.

There it was, a Roman bath, with all the trimmings and the two sisters waiting in their pleated sheer dresses that showed the remainder of their bodies to be admired, their right breast free, the nipple painted, their bodies shaved and scented. They took care of them with pampering massages, then bathing them; shaving off their pubic hair, and this particular ritual aroused them both, following with full body massages and an aroma therapeutic treatment.

"We live like the noble Romans lived," Gord was pleased as punch. He sipped at his cocktail, sitting up and enjoying his foot massage. Joe was lying on his body, asking his pretty hydro-therapist if she would be spending more time doing his back. "I enjoy the art of her hands so much, I feel already being in heaven," he said to Gord.

"This is only the beginning," Gord started his raucous laugh, while Joe sounded like a tomcat being stroked. This was a different type of rejuvenation to the one that saved his life the other night. He stopped comparing it, as the brunette beauty masseuse did well, but he had not yet established any feelings of love with her. "A 'pomp' is a 'pomp'," Gord said in his uncouth way of expressing a sexual act. For Joe it was more. His heart had to be touched, otherwise it was nothing to him and he couldn't climax. But he said nothing to Gord, who meant well. Joe didn't feel though his strength recovering yet. Bathed, shaved, oiled, and massaged they lied down in their short Roman togas to be served a scrumptious meal, with the sisters tending to them, teasing them. The drinking loosened the senses and heightening the senses. The second part of an extensive bacchanal had begun, animating, and the music added to the lapping of the mood, setting the course for an orgy, he saw depicted in Gord's bedroom, where they would eventually retire to celebrate a foursome.

He had not slept well that night waking with nightmares, listening to the voice of Vib. He activated his cellular phone light avoiding to wake his brunette companion, who had worked hard to satisfy all his needs. Carefully he pulled the linen cover back, admired her beautiful back and slipped out of bed. Then he slipped the covers over her lower back again. He left the suite and took a cab. He asked the driver to take him to the Tavern of Iridia, in the Indian City, known to the driver, who sped in a fast, swift drive at night void of any traffic. Joe saw the city's lights and the cupola above the shopping mall of the city, close to the City of Stars.

There were different people in the tavern this time with a different hub. "We change settings and the menu every week," the manager explained handing him a calling card, almost apologetically. "OH," Joe said, "The House of Paradise?" and look astonished at him.

"It's close to here," the waiter said, "you can't miss it. Follow the spice trail." He pointed to the turquoise door with the glass beads. The scent of cinnamon was overpowering to his sense of smell. He entered into a passage and came to Vib's Shop, where he met an assembly of Philippines there, cute, petite, and friendly. They attended to him and he checked on the theme of the night: Thai Special." The young girl attending said "Very nice. Try us. You will not be disappointed." He thanked her. "Another time perhaps." He said, "I was looking for a friend."

"What is her name?" she said.

"Alta," he said and showed her a photograph of a beautiful dusky girl in a tight red dress.

"I cannot say that I have seen her," she said and his heart sank. "But I will ask, wait here." She took the photograph and disappeared through the doorway with the pearl curtain that made a clinking sound as she went through. He sat down on the silver-legged couch, which was covered in a deep-red velvet, and he observed the colourful lampoons that hung from the ceiling. A different set of shelves was arranged at one side of the partitioned room, with many glasses filled with spices. A specially arranged shelving unit was placed closer to the entrance of Vib's Spice Shop. The colour of the spices was reflected in the interior decoration by a skilled decorator.

She came back. "I have spoken to the girls, who knew her. They have prepared a small meal and wish to share it with you...the eldest one could tell you the story." He followed her into the darkened room, decorated with rice-paper and themes from Far-Eastern countries. As soon as he was comfortable the sisters of pleasures appeared. "Don't get up," the one - who he assumed was the eldest one – said, holding him by his hand. She was strong in spite of her delicate hand and long fingers. The lighting changed seamlessly in hues of blue, then changed to pur-ple and dark lacquer-red.

She left and returned with a bottle of rice wine. They toasted. The elder one spoke. The girl next to her trans-lated the elder's talk to him. The rice wine burned down his gullet at first. And then the fire spread like a warm touch from his stomach into all directions. She started translating: "I have to tell you a sad story. Yes, we know Vib. She was running this shop. The day her son married a beautiful young Indian woman and the celebrations con-tinued into the early hours of the morning. In the morning we were alarmed that she had disappeared. The note left behind told us that Ara was kidnapped by a gang of young hoodlums, who demanded a high ransom for her release. The newly-wed husband promised to pay, but he couldn't rise all the cash the kidnappers demanded. She paused.

Mother Vib sold her shop and her son's sister sold her favours to selected customers, who were wealthy. Last month the final payment was needed to have the entire ransom paid off. However, she fell in love with the man with a pony tail, she called him, but as she was too ashamed to ask for a bigger payment, she wanted to talk to him in the morning, but he had left already. Now she is desperate knowing that he would help her, but she cannot find him. It suddenly dawned on Joe that is was him she meant to find. Then he remembered that he had her cel-lular phone number. "Could I see a photograph of Ata?" The girl next to him disappeared again and he took a sip of the Raki, then another – and did not notice that he had emptied half a bottle. "Careful," a voice told him, "you are still on medication." She came back. "This is Ata," she said, "and next to her Alta in the red dress."

"That's her!" He exclaimed.

"Do you know her?" the girl looked astonished.

"Yes, I am the man she is looking for…what is your name?"

"Roi," she said, "but people around here pronounce it 'Roy'. Now Joe remembered, with Roy sitting next to him. He held her, embraced her…

"OK," he cleared his throat. "How much does it all come to?"

"Ten thousand," she said, "dollars."

"All right," he replied, "I pay it all now, and more if needed! Will she live? Is she still alive? What do we know?"

"That is later, I let Vib know."

"Wait!" He said, "you must give me details of the place where she is held. We must know that, on condition that she is alive and shown to us, when we deliver the ransom. I will have to go there alone. It's too dangerous for you."

"Well, yes, perhaps. It is her life on the line."

"You are brave." She kissed him.

"No, I'm not brave. I owe her a debt."

"You love her," she snapped back.

"Perhaps I do, but now is not the time for philosophy, but to save her. I'll phone my friend Gord to help." Joe took his cellular phone from his pocket.

"I will phone Vib to relax now, as help will be on the way."

"Thanks Roy," he said as Gord came online. He told him the ee3me3rgency situation and Gord would help immediately with cash and logistics, besides being part of the action to catch the gang, without taking too great risks to endanger the life of Alta. He promised. He would be ready late morning; pity about the interrupted weekend, but this was an emergency."

"I'll pay for the next one, Gord," he said, listening to Gord's roaring laugh.

"Bring me more wine, Roy, please."

"No," she replies, "first, you ought to be relaxed." She takes him to the change room and she takes his clothes off, complimenting him on his physique, and make him feel well. Then she asks him to lie on the massage table, face down at first, teasing him a bit, followed by the steam room. Speeding up his metabolism to get rid of all the built-up poison in his body, open the pores on his red-dened skin and to clean-out, as she said. She signals him 25 minutes later through the glass door to get a cold shower. He feels like hit by a jolt. Back again on the towel-covered massage table, where she attends to him in a sensual way. He feels another height, this time a short burning, his heart beating like a drum. Then all subsides around him and he's asleep fast.

When he wakes-up again, his clothes are aired and cleaned and hung next to his bed. The room's colours had changed, the new day lets-in soft, clear rays of an ivory light through the shutters. He showers and dresses. Roy is greeting him kissing his cheeks, taking him through to breakfast. She's dressed in black leather gear. "I'll come with you," she says business like. "It is all arranged."

"No," he replies, "I'll go alone."

"Well, only I know the way," she says with a smirk at the edges of her lips. "You have the cash to worry about. It arrived this morning by courier from Gord."

"All right," he's now calm, "when?"

"We have to leave in twenty minutes. I drive."

"OK." He tucks into his oats and fruit she had arranged for their breakfast. He looks into Roy's eyes and he feels her warmth of friendship and love held back for now. Having finished he gets up: "By the way," he draws her close, hugs her, "thank you my friend and lover for yesterday. You are magnificent with your fingers and lips." Roy smiles her mysterious smile: "You taste nice, no wonder Alta loves you."

"Thank you. I'm blessed with friends and lovers," he muses and then speaks softly to her. She turns, opens the door business-like and steps through it with her face being pale and serious. He follows gazing at her cat-like walk. She is sensual like all the girls here, but still has her own characteristic way of walking. She has her tight leather gear on and looked an attractive Amazon worrier. Her short top covered with a leather jacket sat on her hip pants. He couldn't entirely recollect his image of her other than slim and lithe, an aesthetical delight of a perfectly toned body. Everything was slim about her, save for her full lips. He wondered if she had them treated to appear as her most prominent feature that drew an immediate response to be kissed by them.

She drove well, maybe a bit too fast. "You have to switch on the navigation system, Roy," as she was unsure about an unknown fork in the road. It worked wonders. He looked at her destination she had thus to give away.

"I'm not supposed to do this," she moaned, as she typed the name of destination into the gadget, "but I trust you Joe," she said and he nodded: City of the Sun and Moon outbuildings...IMPOSSIBLE - He felt struck by lightning. But as Roy had not mentioned anything, he pretended not having seen their destination and their respective coordinates. His mind worked feverishly to transfer this info to Gord, if his standby supposed to be of any help. Roy was driving uphill with the entrance gate to the city's walls that were gigantic like Babylon's. At the gate she had to accompany the guard to sign-in at the office. Joe used her absence to send Gord an SMS-message with the coordinates of the meeting place and the name; he saw on the navigation-screen, he was familiar with. He warned Gord to stay back at a safe distance.

Roy appeared just at the time when he pocketed his mobile phone. "All in order," she said, "It's a new shift and they had to check." She parked her Merc in a specific area in close proximity to the general staff quarters. There was still a walk on foot further. Joe hoped that Gord would have information through a sensor, Joe imagined that he had added to the suitcase when adding the cash, but he himself had no knowledge about. He could not remember having read anything to that regard in his notes to him.

They walked to the back of the staff quarters and through a small and unmanned black gate into the semi-desert, which stretched out between the city and the hills beyond. He was glad he had put on his suede ankle boots and his jeans. Roy must be hot in her leather gear. At a distance he noticed the agreed place, a few huts that served as an oasis for the hunters and animals that were fed there by the game wardens, outside the hunting season, Roy explained to him. "Stop now, Joe," she said extending her left hand touching him. "We have to wait until we get permission to pass this thorn tree."

"I see a torch," he said.

"That's the signal, let's access slowly now." She had taken her jacket off, as probably a sign that all what was agreed was now on. Jo clutches his briefcase that has a secret lock fitted, which he activates, just as Gord had told him. It activated a honing device and would deactivate the money inside, when the bag is opened, once had let go of it. He wonders what else Gord had devised, what he hadn't told him about. He mustn't think of the money inside and he wishes that all's over fast, or the will be all dead. In Africa this is a dangerous game, as there's not much value on a person's life. He is adamant to request to see Alta first, he tells Roy.

Alta appears as soon as they reach the low fence of the Kraal. Roy has to stay behind, while Joe has to place the suitcase into the centre of the round area in front of a ron-davel, in the axis of their access. He approaches with the same speed as Alta is moving towards him. He places the suitcase into the centre of the Kraal and only then he let go of the secret lock as Alta is next to him. That's the signal. He pulls Alta to the ground in a sudden stumble: "Down Alta, down," he whispers. The first shot rings out. The perplexed young guy with the baklava, who came out behind Alta, reaches for the suitcase and runs away with it and with another guy. Some pursue him, more shots are fired and he falls. He had seen Roy duck to the ground, as he is holding Alta's arm. The fighting is short and fierce at the back of the rondavels. Dirt, dust, and piece of wood are flying about into the hot air in a cloud, as if an army had attacked. Then there's stillness and suddenly familiar voices are heard.

"Joe, Joe?" Gord calls.

"Yes," Joe said, "yes, here!" Gord charges ahead with his white teeth glistening in the sun. He smiles like a successful warlord holding a shotgun.

"All OK?" Joe gets up and helps Alta to her feet, whose body had been covered by his own. "Are you all right Alta love?" She circles his waist albeit she's in shock, not wanting to let go.

"Who was that brown faced man?" Gord asks.

"An Indian man?" Joe asks Gord.

"The man with the khaki outfit?" Gord muses, then continues: "Someone shouted his name, Ray or something like that."

"Ray? Sounds like Raj. Do you know him?

"I saw his face with one corner of my eye, as he charged after the youngster with the baklava, who had the money and he shot him. You see he is now a killer too." Gord is curious about his concern, still with half a smirk on his face.

"Indeed," Joe said, "indeed! But now all this makes sense. It's a long story."

"Where is he? Is he the man behind the kidnapping?"

"My uncle," said Alta and she is shaking.

"I never saw him. NO!" Joe shouts. "He came to cash the booty."

"He has touched me a few times, but I couldn't see his face," Alta gasps, "I hate him!"

"OK, OK, relax now Alta. We will get him, don't worry." Gord smiles again showing his white teeth. "I have him well covered. He'll be leading us to his secret hiding place with all the cash. By the time he sees the suitcase empty and the few hundred dollars destroyed, we will have him. His dark helpers are dead, except for one, whom we will question now. I have called John, a friend from a detective bureau, who officially investigates the case. We assist him."

As John arrives, Gord introduces him and he starts taking all the contact numbers and data. "Where is Roy?" Joe suddenly is missing her. "She's all right," Gord said, "she has been shot at, but fortunately it's only a flesh wound. She was lucky. My helper took her to the hospital. Bck to the Roman village then," Gord said.

"I'll drive her car," Joe tells Gord, who has to finish some talk with Joe and the will join the others.

"Are you all right Alta?" Joe asks her as she settles next to him in Roy's car. She leans against him, kissing him and cuddling up to him. Joe drives carefully to the village.

"Take this," he hands her a few tablets, the doc gave him after he recovered from his accident. Joe hands her his water flask and she swallows the tablets. By the time he arrives at the village, she has dozed-off. He stops the car, walks over to her side, and opens the door for her. She stirs and he helps her out. "I wash up first," she said, "and then we lie down a bit together." He prepares her a bath and then he helps her undressing. Alta is still shaking a bit at times, as in a fever. He could see red marks on her skin, caused by ties around her ankles and her wrists that are swollen. He helps her into the bath and she wishes him to soap and wash her. He undresses and steps into the warm water. It's his care she'll need to recover quickly. "Let's for now talk about us," she utters, as she lies back and he holds her. Her head above water, she loves to float outstretched. He massages her ankles and her wrists. They emerge from the bath and he dries her wrapping her into a huge towel, using another to dry her. They sit on her bed and he holds her in his arms. She wishes to kiss him and she slides over him and his arousal.

They wake-up in the middle of the night, as Alta had a nightmare. He calms her. As they tire again, he switches the light off. In the morning she wakes him, having again straddled him. She's alive. How could you refuse her on grounds of tiredness? He muses. He is delighted with her and they make love again. Alta is suddenly back into her state as he knows her. The medication he gave her helped her like magic. She'll go to an examination later. For now all she wants is his love.

He wakes. It is winter. He is in Africa, his home by choice. There is stillness. Not one soul. All is well, it seems, no more nightmares, no night sweat. His phone rings. It's Alta: "I will be free this weekend, will you come?"

"Yes," he said, "I'll fetch you Friday afternoon. How is Vib?"

"She is fine. She has bought the shop back and I help her."

"Uncle Raj?"

"Raj? Well, he has left the country. Gord let him go, as soon as he had found all the stolen money. He earned a bonus, but he asked only for his expenses though. OK, don't worry too much, I'll get even with him. Thank you Joe."

She takes me into her arms, as soon as I enter Vib's Spice Emporium. The sweetness from her body washes over me.

"You know it's Vib?"

"What?"

"It's Vib he loved more than anybody else."

"Really?"

"Yes, he used her when she was small."

"Abuse?"

"In a way, yes, coerced her into satisfying him. He was expelled from his family. That had hurt him deeply and Vib took him into her shop. He was always good to us, but he had a dark side that pricked his inside like a thorn, finally overpowering him. Now I go back to Vib and her spice shop, but for lovers I only take you. She kissed him again.

Astra

Zanec has lost his friend and his access to a city he loved. The magic of the place had shut-down like a light, shut-down to him when there's hardly any connection left, no continuation of the work he had once begun and thrived-in. It's tragic, but who notices?

Every time he arrives at the airport, he is still trying to contact her, but there's stillness on the other end of the line. It rings and rings and there is no reply. This is a dead end; nobody will come to see him, when he arrives at the airport. He is restless and he needs to find another soul, someone who has equally lost connection to a life that'll offer the full way of past experiences, the mature sensual touch and the key to an earthly happiness that has been lost since a long time to him.

Only poets have the key, poets, who are the sensors of a fine web of emotions that lie below the surface of a city's skin, below the agglomeration of places filled with treasures, nobody can see. Hidden by layers upon layers of the lives of at least hundred generations and the richness of souls that lived here and who are still present, but only to few genuine people with the magical touch, who listen to those voices that speak to them suddenly, unexpectedly, and from their deep inside.

Zanec is moving across a new, unknown city. Its ancient places and walls of enclosure are magical and often appear to be out of place. He has found by sheer accident a house of pleasures and a young woman inside, who'll see him at once. He falls in love with her. She's not like any other woman in such places, not like any woman he had ever met. Thrown by fate into a place of courtesans, she entertains the intellectuals and high-powered personalities. She has though taken an interest in Zanec. They are matching well and are comfortable with each other. This happiness grows on them. It becomes impossible for him to stay away from her. Only once he had arrived to a late appointment; she didn't want to put him off and Stella was worn-out that night in spirit, and she did not wish to continue with her lucrative, but soul-erosive profession. In spite of it all she was cheerful, as he always evokes a pleasant nature in her immediately. Zanec takes her home and cares for her with a warm bath, washing her gently, pampering her body and make her feeling good. She falls asleep in his arms, never wishing to go anywhere else, but remain in this love, and not in the trickery of making strangers feel loved, which is a great illusion she had sold successfully.

"Enough of all this sexual illusion," she exclaims, "love is all she'll need."

"Indeed?" He replies in a soft tone, "but we all have dreams and live a life filled with illusions at the side." They have a disagreement and Zanec wishes to avoid a domestic life that will be hackneyed for love and sex, and that will kill the magical way of life they enjoy together right now.

The next morning he arrives at the Pleasure Palace and she is gone. Whereto? He asks. Nobody seems to know, not even her best friend Jenn. In a state of desperation he returns home worrying all the way about his short temper having criticised her. He notices that he always takes the same route across the Square with the one uneven corner, past the old palace that crumbles, followed by the boisterous new section of the city, where the haste and speed have outdone a peaceful and tranquil life, leaving no space for an inner dialogue, but always the same wish for renewable goods that have no meaning and no relationship for happiness. He seeks something that is powerful, a tool that helps him to find Stella. Whatever that tool is, he has just to believe in it strongly and it'll turn-up as a key to his and her happiness.

The next morning, after a bad night filled with a series of horrid dreams, all seems to him to be suddenly different. All has changed! He gets up, washes, dresses, and is on his way. As he comes across the Square he realizes it is not the same Square it used to be. Even daylight reflects from low clouds, as if the sun would enjoy filtering her rays through a foggy atmosphere. A surge of voices meets him from all the souls who live here once, a murmuring and moaning continues, occasionally an outcry. He rushes to the Pleasure Palace as usual, across this uneven Square where the patterns on the floor are lit-up like a magical board game, in bright green and blue spots with ivory-white in between. He's never seen it so clean. Is he transported into other times, like a carnival happening? He muses.

People are dressed in strange costumes, long-nosed and sombre staring at him; only his disguise seems to be different. His dress colours changed to charcoal, rather than black, with a dark-brown tint of sepia, the ink he likes to write with, the ink Stella had given him as a present, filled into a pen with a golden nib and a delightful lightness in one's hand. He recalls when they had met, she wished to be drawn by him, a portrait, he created in many different wondrous ways that gave her pleasure and thrills, especially as she dropped her clothes for him to be depicted like Maya, in the nude. It was as if he had touched her all the time, pen stroke by pen stroke. Suddenly in his being were all the faces that had touched her, and he felt all the desires that went towards her from all the men she had seen, were now all his alone that would touch her. He was HER man.

He took his notebook and sat down on a bench at the city's great park that stretched between the old one and the new extension, where the president's home was situated, close by. He saw the palace only once, strolling past with her on a Sunday afternoon. Her free day when they visited an art museum and enjoyed all the surrounding beauty he showed her. She had never realized its presence in such abundance around her. He could show it to her like a wizard shows things on a computer program. He shared it all with her.

As he had noted his thoughts down, he heard a clap of thunder and saw the arc of lightning highlighting the ancient buildings in front of him, he had never noticed hurrying past them on his way to Stella's Pleasure Palace that looked like an arcade of columns, with a fountain placed in its courtyard featuring a rock face with angels and nymphs playing in its cascading waters.

Now here, here is the place that had opened-up to him, he must though look at it carefully, as he is drawn immediately to another small, but magical palazzo that sucks him in. And the heavens had opened-up and he seeks refuge in an old courtyard – the place seemed to be desolate and antiquated – untouched by human hands for a long time. But in all walls and the small internal square an aura of energy and power is present. His senses are affected most effectively.

All of a sudden Stella's face appears. She beckons him, like a spook to follow her. His heart races and he cries out: "Stella!" But no sound leaves his paralyzed lips. He rushes after her: "Wait Stella! Wait!" Neither does she hear him, nor does she slow down. She gives-off signs with her arms and hands, pointing fingers. He follows her in a blind rush to reach her, but he cannot. Although he is desperate by now, he is filled with a thrill of adventure and exploration, the two elements that make his life worth living. But it's Stella who loves him, the motor that brings all to life, even old and ancient places, like this palazzo. But in the heat of his rush he might have hurt her. She fades away and he panics.

Then a hand touches his shoulder, it's her. She kisses him fleetingly indicating to him that he should follow, her finger closing her lips – he has to be quiet, just believe! He recalls her words from before: "Trust me!" He does, but he is on a trip to nowhere, he thinks. After a few corners there's a labyrinth where he feels completely lost. There's silence, darkness, and a flash of lightning which reveals her slender arm and hand. It's a right hand and it's AyAy's and he has to touch it. As he does, her hand turns to stone. He can feel the cold of its touch with a tinge of warmth, a sign that she's been here just now and he had missed her. He senses the imprint of her and surges of his emotional being recall in him the ancient rhymes: Touch the Blarney Stone…, but like this? He presses his hand into the mould and it's exactly his hand, fitting so accurately with the way his palm sits on the mould. His whole bod starts shaking loaded with electric current. Like a lightning strike it races through his veins. He thinks to die and turn to ashes and he cries out her name: A, Ay, AyAy…for three times.

Sounds of thunder reverberate through walls and all will fall and turn to dust. He stands alone in the midst of the Square with one unequal corner and in the fountain in the centre that holds his naked body. He has started to shiver, yet nobody has noticed him there, except for one white dove, who has flown in to his side and sits like a toy on his shoulder. She coos. "What?" He could hear AyAy's voice: "just point to yourself, wishing clothes, and you will be clothed." He points his finger to his body and wishes an Armani suit for himself. But instead, he is clothed into something like feathered pieces, looking like a giant bird from paradise. He sings and whistles, in his hand he finds a beautiful mouth organ. He immediately begins to play a tune: La Paloma, and the white dove starts to sing. People gather around and throw coins to this unusual pair of artists, Bird-man and white dove? From now on he is known as the 'Bird-man' and wherever he'll go money flows.

He calls-out for AyAy, but she's away, nowhere to be found. All his income he'll save for her, so she could by her home, her palazzo, if that'll bring relief: That palazzo which disappeared and has fallen to dust, she could re-build that one that gave him his magical life turning into a bird-man. Yet he travels and enjoys cities.

One night AyAy appears in his dreams telling him about his powers to fly. The white dove talks to him in the morning: "Just point your index finger at a distance, wish you were there, and you'll be. I'll come with you." And as he points his index finger to the top of the dome, he flies and lands with his white dove there, using his index finger to navigate.

The people are amassing everywhere, spending their coins appreciating their songs, and the growing masses cannot get enough from the incredible, unique, and exquisite pair of entertainers, who express their happiness vocally. "This is after all a wonderful life," he tells Paloma, "but I need to find AyAy, don't you agree?" Paloma nods: "You just have to believe in it." He flies about the whole town, to all places of great interest, squares and monuments. Everywhere the pair will attract crowds and induces merriment, but he himself has no happiness at present, with AyAy gone. But where is she? He hadn't seen her face since his hand had touched the magical stone, except in his numerous dreams. Now he's living a life in luxury and in every thinkable way of gaining riches, he does not want, but her. AyAy is what he wants in life, but life has taken her in her prime. Now whatever he seeks, nobody is interesting enough for him, and nobody can help him. He comes across Mount Ida and an old wise man who lives in a hut nearby. He usually leads tourists to the birth place of Zeus. That's where he intends to go and see if it offers him some clues. The old man just shakes his head, he cannot talk being death and dumb. He points to a picture that has been taken at his place. That one he knows, he has taken one with his magical lens, a mere pointing of his finger: It is showing AyAy. This time she is sitting on a tripod above a slot in the ground, with steam vapours rising. "Delphi, the oracle?" he mumbles having not been there and the old man smiles. He shows him a slide-show and the pictures are all of AyAy. It shows her and him and AyAy as a child, and he realizes that it is his child. Paloma tells him it is his daughter that came forward from the temple of his head. It's like a tale in mythology, but not everything is a tale.

Zanec rushes off to fly to Delphi. He finds the sacred place and the sanctuary of ancient times. For a moment he recreates the temple of Apollo and all statues of worriers. The domain bustles with people. He seeks out Pythia's help. She is in trance, yet she greets him back.

"Welcome Zanec."

"Thanks and my respects," he said and he can see AyAy in her facial features, but she keeps her eyes closed.

"You must touch me," she said to him. He approaches closely, his fingers touch her face carefully, as he strokes her. The vapours carry him away with her and he sees himself lying with AyAy making love.

The mountain grumbles, then moves with cracking sounds. The gods are angry, rocks loosen and fall. She covers his body with hers and they escape unscathed. All around is laid to ruins and dust clouds still rise and waft towards the valley. As soon the dust clouds have lifted he finds himself to be alone. He must have lost his magical powers, he muses. An old woman, dressed in black, cowers on the remaining steps of the destroyed temple. He addresses her in his shock.

"Have you found AyAy?"

"Well," she said, "you must firstly access the caverns below the temple. But don't forget to take your white dove with you."

"But Paloma is gone," he said.

"No," the woman replied, "she is not! Just wish for her to come back." As he thinks of his wish, Paloma settles on his shoulder.

"See?" She hollers, "that's the only magic still left. Use it wisely and you'll find AyAy." Then he turns to look at the entrance to the caverns. As his gaze returns to the steps, the old woman is gone. He recalls that she was all the time knitting holding a thread, she used to cut at intervals.

He prepares to descend to the caverns. "Stay with me my love-bird," he talks sweetly to Paloma...

"I will guide you now my friend," she answers, filling his heart with renewed hope. Will he find AyAy? YES, he recalls the old woman's voice: If you believe strongly, you will!

*

Big Apple Flight

He came towards his desk with a rising inner unrest, just as a dull and steady rain had set-in again since a day, stirring up humidity levels and its rising drew on his nerves, shit! He sat down at his PC and tried another round on work already set-up, indexing his vast amount of writings, which grew steadily since the days of Ann, and now even more so. He searched for specific words to express his love he had felt and could not wonder enough about her gift of a craft she had opened up in him. A craft that had magically been extracted from within his being.

This to him seemed to be a power beyond anybody's control, a magical wand with which she had stroked his obelisk, called Cleopatra's Needle. And he recalled the times he wanted to meet her there, hold her hand and walk along the Thames on a warm afternoon that would always end-up in one of the numerous pubs, where they sat close together for a drink, some food, whatever they could think of doing together. He felt free, unbridled, and fit for free living, let float and carry-on this butterfly-state of being. Let the thoughts drift like flotsam on the sea. Let the mind be at rest on her generous bosom everybody wanted to touch and dive into, find the ultimate answer to their pleasures. He came close to it once, twice, and the third time she withdrew. Had she attracted him like a bird is attracted to the sweet scent of a flower's beaker, he knew he could only dip his beak into the honeyed pot if she would come to terms with his status-quo: Being a poet, but at the same time not entirely free. He was never one to be possessed by virtues of a contract, he despised. He was free as a child and golden in hip-appearance, a young Alexander made for adventure in love, emptying the 'Cup of Plenty' every time he found an exuberant counterpart in love. Life was wonderful and women beautiful in the moment of truth and an intimate touch. That was all. Then he had to leave and search for something he could never have: Was it for endless thrills of love?

It had not always been like this. Just one unrequited love had set him off flying: Once Icarus had been warned by Daedalus, when fitted out with his invention of feathers that were held in place by wax, not to fly too high towards the sun and not too low to touch the sea. And having fallen in love to be turned blind, warned by his elders, he could not see the path of reason, as love had blocked all his senses. But this was the perfect path, he was on now, or what? He followed his instincts, like a bird, a butterfly, and the forging of a lover thus began. Although she had abandoned him, he still loved her. Even her girlfriend noticed this, but then nobody else was on his side. He had to abandon his love that had made him go through all motions, and that time he had learned yet controlling his time to a climax. He can still see her face and he can still hear her voice with which she had captivated him, besides melt his heart with her radiating smile. Cupid's arrows had penetrated deeper than just below his skin.

Then she came. This woman, he had known since she was 15, had just turned 18, pretty and self-assured. She is on and off meeting him, just as she had switched on the lights of attraction, to turn them off again. Now she's in her twenties, and he thought of meeting her again. Eventually, if she will be still curious about him and his potential love he could give her, she'll meet him. She came into his life when all seemed to him a senseless existence, though love never was a dead end to him: the only remaining bastion against the lies and the all-devouring onslaught of human greed. In this one door she had opened, the one she had placed her strong hand on its lever, he never knew he had any longer access to. She was the one, he thought, he could trust from then on.

In a way, it is as if life has already drawn-up a schedule that we seem to follow now and then consciously. But this happened to be a track he followed intuitively and by sheer gut feel. It was though his heart that sensed these feelings of being seduced. Then again, he thought that it would be all just a great ride on the fantasy bus. But why not enjoy the ride?

She came into his life repeatedly, at intervals, as if she would be his only girlfriend from the times back on the ranch. They never had stopped to play games that continued from their children's minds to become more inquisitive and then growing into more than just a skin-flick-slide. However, she decided about her own ways of dealing with a future, and he had found a bus ride that took him through strange lands, with someone lending him a hand and sharing a kiss. While accompanying him she showed him new ways of seeing things around him and to look at life and love. She gave him all she had in unbridled ways, he never found before. Perhaps he became more conscious of what he had: It was the gift of love that heals and closes the wounds made by others, one being pure and rare. Is this magic? A miracle?

It also became his immediate experience with death, he had not thought about at all. This time he had no personal brushes with the hooded dark skeletal shadow, but with another woman, sensual and full of life. Whatever we all will think of her, she was a human being and her own philosophical outlook on life jelled with his: Love of music, passion for the arts, and above all the 'Sacred Places' of antiquity. How did this fusion ever become such an important milestone in his life?

Lost in deep thoughts about love and betrayal, virtual plays and fornication, he looked for answers from within his heart. Would he fall for its betrayal? It had betrayed him often before. As long as something good will come out of all this, she had said, but he had no space in his mind for such moralistic talk now, having become focuses entirely on responses of her sexual craftiness. She had become a drug for him, an obsession. Fate had ruled this, she believed, to be a unique experience and he had a notion of it being the great one in his life.

But she had found spiced-up solace in the arms of her girlfriend and he had found Ellen to be a friend, a true counterpart of a good-looking young woman with her share of life's knocks and pleasures. He found with her healthy sexual tension and refreshing thought, brilliance of memories and sky-rides of erotic fantasies. There was suddenly everything he had missed for a long time. However, she was above the world's outer mask of being, and he was straight and a man. He wished to love her as intense as possible and take in return all she could offer him. He had once told her that he wanted her. Now there had been a good indication of one moment, when he felt turned-on by her. He appreciated her.

He wrote her many sketches of his thoughts, painting them like drawings, at times like portraits of her. Stories poured out of his head and the poet had come unshackled again. She had always been a Muse to him, but recently she turned him on with her visual appearance. Then he would instantly conceive a story with such ease, it would stir him into a height. Her smile, her movements, her being and her loyalty mixed with that shot of female curiosity had him going for her. They walked together for a while to the bus stop along the way.

He found himself riding a bus, as she had decided to stay at home this time. It was a different bus, he had to climb the steep steps to get to the deck. This one had strange voices inside, greetings he recognized from a stay before. He heard the person in front of him asking the conductor for a ticket to Athens. She sounded like Athina. However, he asked for the same type of ticket. There was a shout: Hah! Someone being angry at the front. It echoed through the bus. A stocky man in a gym-shirt had entered the bus from the front entrance and had an exchange of silly words with the driver. Another person entered the discussion, then another, and then all passengers in the bus became involved. A young woman with auburn hair to her shoulders, who sat at the window seat ahead of him, turned her head facing him: "I gather you cannot understand what was happening in front there?"

"No," he said, "but if you could tell me, I'll listen to you." She spoke good English and she explained to him the dispute of the man and the driver: The man entering the bus had accused the driver for being late today, but the driver did not respond. The man flexed his muscles and intimidated the driver, scalding his attitude. As he carried on with a verbal fight, the bus driver got up from his seat and left, telling him that it's his bus and he can do as he likes. People took sides, as they all had to go to work, fearing that they would be late and being scolded for matters beyond their own fault. The conductor jumped from the bus to fetch the driver from the café next door and began to act as peace-maker, smoking a cigarette with him and settle the debate. Finally both returned and the bus moved on. The noisy debates between the passengers subsided. The odd murmuring remained like an after-quake, surfacing now and then.

Zanec thanked the talkative woman, who translated him the happening from Greek into English. She looked pretty and as he observed, had a colour-matching habit in her dressing and accessories. She sensed that she had roused his interest and she turned her torso sideways, as if she would model for him. He edged closer to her. Even her watch strap matched. He asked her if she was reading Classical literature. She said she was reading it in Greek and not in English. Then it was her turn to throw in a few words to the driver that she wished to exit at the next stop. He could no longer ask her for her name, as she rose from her seat in a flash. For a short moment he could see the bus stop's name, while she disembarked through the front door. Her words reverberated in him: This is typical in Greece. He had asked her if this row had been finished and she replied that it is never finished. Before he could reply with another sentence, coming and going people had blotted out her face and appearance, and he felt that their conversation had been just as unfinished as the debate of angry people before, cut short by moving on with business. A great pity she had to leave, as he could not ask for her telephone number, as he longed for a longer conversation with her.

It had been indeed an interesting experience of tension and a sudden eruption of pent-up anger spreading through the bus, affecting everyone and yet not causing havoc, perhaps a relief from the slog of everyday commuting to work, and the suppressed freedom of being a slave of one's work. Maybe part of it had to do with the morning's sexual tension that had not yet been released by the culprit who started the stir, being oversensitive that morning.

*

Bluebeard

Joan and I walk the pavements and seek to be alone, but have to always warn the group of friends, when someone from them decides to come unexpectedly, especially to disrupt their opening G-Man's Car Games. The vintage model which is always dumped, never show up an outdated Jaguar – we both like. So, Karl is the right person, to start the one, Joan has still available in her backyard. We drive to the West, the trendy set and the Now-generation of fakers and users, who roam the streets of Jozy and its empty off-ramp boulevards, where Highway robbers keep a vigil for an ailing modern car.

I like Joan and it's the only time I can be alone with her, while her spouse steals cars to get them moving, as she says, feeling sorry for them that they are all abandoned, victims of the New-Age rust that was non-existent for many years here previously, but now it all came back with a vengeance, like HIV-AIDS and any pandemic, a violent virus, we are lucky enough to stay clear of. Joan wants me to be close to her, as she wishes to be touched, and in choosing me, she is confident to be safe and treated the way a sensual woman wishes to be treated by her man. That is Joan, living perhaps in bygone times, appreciative of sex without stimulant drugs, natural and wanted, experiencing her own level of feelings, living to free her emotions in climaxes that Dan, her spouse does not appreciate and he is even less inclined to understand. Besides, Dan the bully, has chosen himself above all others to be a leader. He leads by intimidation and fear he impresses onto others, not by means of an authority due to his abilities and talents. He does oppress others in his own fear of failure, in order to thrive as the only one on top of the pops, telling all their grave mistakes, enforcing them to work for him and to be content with the left-over milk he hands them to feed on, while he will gather greedily all the cream. Staff and contemporary co-workers call him behind his back: 'The Ayatollah-Dan'. They call him a dictator. I call him a monster. His oldest daughter calls him 'Bluebeard'.

Perhaps he treats just like that, but he is cautious to me, even reserved, an actor to play a lion in his lair to get me in a moment I've lost my alertness, offering him an easy prey. I am aware of it and he knows.

I like his younger daughter May. She is like a serene dove; betrothed to John, soon to be married. She is keen to go and leave Bluebeard's castle. Then there is Lee. She is sensitive, an artist and sensual at times, and unexpectedly rebellious. She makes constantly noises, imitating Bluebeard's behaviour in her way, exaggerating his moves and cocky attitude. Her favourite act is to talk about Henry VIII, as if Bluebeard would compare himself to him and being acceptable as a monster, stature, cock, and all. Joan is used to these egotistical performances that had become hackneyed repetitions for her, now that she had lived through that as his spouse. She loves to drop into her cooing her most sweet inner secrets, but every time we come near a tete-a-tete, the bully Dan will charge.

Henry VIII will take his two-edged sword to cut us both into pieces. He, the powerful bully, now ridiculously small and divested from his entire sexual prowess and his constant show-off pushing people out of his way, who are physically weaker, is an ugly dwarf. The high-minded monster who spreads fear amongst the guild of creative artists, the Bluebeard of his family. Only Lee calls him those names and he seems to respect her, even fear her. She is uncouth in his presence, in words and her demeanour, probing him with lewd slang words, she throws at him in her attempt to keep him at bay. She wishes to avoid him stepping across the threshold of her aura, even if she stirs his feelings as a man, dressing in sheer clothes and loose, tight tops, avoiding the use of underwear. Lee loves to be sadistic, keeping him horny and tease him to the point of boil. She shows him a frontage he dislikes, but Lee, who is Carol with her real name, is in danger of being thought of as a libertine by their servants, especially their black gardener with the indented mark of a knife attack on his head. He works closely to Lee's room peeking into her bathroom window, building strong desires to fuck her.

One day I had to come to Bluebeard's castle to be present at his preview of great vintage cars, he wished to show off and impress me with. He took me along and warned me though about his giant dog, a Newfoundland beast, who rolled across everything and everybody in his way, like a steam roller gone mad. I thought: "Just do it and we'll see!" I was received by Joan, still in her revealing nightgown that flowed around her slightly luxuriant body. I had not seen her before in such sheer and revealing clothes, being drawn to her immediately. The silly Bluebeard-boss wanted to get me into one of his vintage models and drive to a spot some hours away. "But that's in midst of an African bush," Joan cried-out, "how can you even think of that?" I didn't either know the nearby town, nor did I have any liking to drive with him there.

I greeted Joan kissing her cheeks and hugging her. She must have felt the vigorous reactions from my body towards her, woken up to greet her, telling her about my feelings. "We have to have breakfast," she announced, "we have a guest!" With that announcement the serving woman hurried to set the table. Joan poured coffee for me and we talked about recent plays and the arts. I liked talking to Joan, as she had a broad range of interests, always updating on any news. She was sensitive to the latest expressions of an exhibition of Erotic art. "Let's go to the exhibition then," she said, "and enjoy the genre." I nodded. "It would be interesting," I said.

"You wanted to paint our portraits," she mentioned, takings a sip of coffee.

"Yes, I recall that. I'd love to do it now...but..."

"That would be fine," she said, "come with me." Joan sat down in her favourite chair in the room adjoining her bedroom and she loosened her top that parted to reveal her beautiful, almost child-like breasts. She saw herself in the mirror on the opposite wall, adjusted her loose night-gown again and then offered one of her breasts openly to my view. I started sketching her. "Wait," she said, as she got up again to lock the door. At that moment Dan, the giant, stormed into her room, annoyed that he was supposed to drive alone to Dingaanshoek, and I supposed to come with him now. There was a sloshing trampling sound. The huge dog charged unexpectedly from behind, ignoring all in his path of attack and he was striking hard: Bam, bam, and Dan's legs folded below him, his giant frame came crushing down backwards to the floor with his head first. He was knocked out, lying still. Joan called his valet to come immediately. He appeared with a helper and they placed him on a carrier to take him to his quarters.

Dan was out of their way now, rendered out of action for the time being. Joan called the doctor, who would be able to pass by late at night, or rather in the morning. "Fuck," somebody shouted. "Fuck!" It was Carol-Lee who screamed and came close to me. "Fuck!" She took her top off to reveal her excited nipples. She rubbed them and screamed like a bungee rushing through the passages of the castle. Joan was pale, placing her hands on her gown, after Carol had left. She opened her top and let her silken cloth slide from her shoulders, but she still held the gown in front of her, crossed at her thighs. I just sat still and sketched.

After some time, when the noise had abated, she stood up, came to join me close-by and sat down in my lap, offered me her lips and then her body. I took her into my arms, she was shaking. I kissed her. Slowly she relaxed. Then the door opened and Joan's youngest daughter, May, appeared. She was aching on some food that was stuck in her throat. Joan placed her gown over her. "Zorky is painting me," she apologized and fetched some tweezers. I asked May to open her mouth and I saw a thread that must have been left in the chicken breast from stitching the filling in. "I will remove it for you, if you'll hold still."

It took me a few seconds. I got hold of the end of the thread and pulled it out gently. She coughed and had to bring up, soiling my top and pants. "Oh, I'm sorry," she stammered. "I felt ill suddenly, let me wash you off." May pulled me to the bathroom and asked me to take my clothes off. "I'll bring you some jeans and a top from my wardrobe, from my friend, he's your size." She said and disappeared. I took my pants off and then my top, waiting for her to hand me clothes.

"Oh she said, you are naked. You look good. Are you doing any sports?"

"Yes, I do some walking and now and then I hit a golf ball."

"Oh great," she said, taking my soiled clothes. "Mom will be happy to have you," she kissed my cheeks turning a gentle pink. "You must take her now, or I will take you!"

"Oh," I said, "with pleasure my dear May, you are indeed beautiful." She looked at my cock as I slipped into the jeans.

"You do not have underwear?"

"No, I don't like any." She smiled. "You are a different man to the ones we know around here…Take her now, take her now…" she sang and disappeared into the dark passage quickly.

I went to Joan's room. She stood there against the window. She was naked. The sun was illuminating her body and burnt a halo around her. I took my top off and moved close to her caressing her from behind. She fitted well into my body. I could feel her heartbeat rising as I cupped her breasts. She turned her head around and we kissed. It was the warmth of the sun and Joan's love that melted into me. She turned around as she kissed me back, then opened the waist button on my jeans, inserted her hand and caressed my cock. I had my hand behind her left buttock and the other one holding her upper body tightly against mine. We kissed deeper. Her tongue was hot and spreading into my entire mouth. Joan was in heat. Then she took me by my hand and pulled me to her bedroom.

She knelt down and took my pants off. My penis snapped into an upright position, as she freed it from the generous garb. She cupped my balls and caressed me gently. I felt the tips of her teeth on my bursting crown.

"Falling in love with you again," I said.

"Let me taste you," she said. In the light-blue and white atmosphere, our pink bodies gleamed in the filtered light. Joan wanted me to lie down, be passive for a while. She started tasting me and kiss my entire body. I was aroused completely, my skin sensitive to her slightest touches.

"I want to come doing that to you," she said. As she rubbed her clit against my crown, she came.

"Oh, oh! I come…please fuck me now," she cried and fell over me, moving in and out of me in her straddled pose. "Ah! Ah." She could hardly stop, as I moved against her…

Then she was still and it was my time to taste her. I was into her neck and breasts, as she asked me to suck her nipples. "You do it right, but when I signal you, bite them, not too hard though!"

"I love them, Joan, they are like your daughter's."

"Oh, Carol's," she said, "yes, we have a similarity in bodies and mine is not as slim."

"No, you are beautiful, just great, wonderful, and slightly luxuriant with that decadent edge to it." Joan laughed.

"You are complimenting me too much, I love it all…Oh, I feel horny now…oh, touch me." I placed my fingers into her and she moaned, rubbing against them. The cautious first moves of our lovemaking turned into a furious twisting now. I still had a magical angle of restraint in me and wished to bring Joan to her climax, as many times as I possibly could.

Out of the blue she turns-on like a true French woman, and she wanted to experience all the moves she had talked and dreamed about, as we slid from straight phys-ical to oral sex. It was a great fuck indeed, as we could oscillate our want to bring-out the animal in us at times. Then, as she could bring me to the edge, she wanted me to ride her from the back, as she closed her legs tightly to give me more friction, while she burst with sap of her juices. I was climbing into the back of her and with my legs on the bed, she pushed hard into me and cried: "More Zorky, my sweet fucky, more! More! More! Ah! .Now! Come with me now – UHH!" And she started howling and I knew that could not stop now and had to hold back, but I had passed the point of no return. "I'll come now Joanie, I come sweetly, spreading all my love into you!"

"Yes. Yes. Yes!" she cried, "fuck, more, fuck…fuck – Ahh! Ohh! Ahh! I am dying …with you…Zorky.-"

We had such heat in our bodies that we could hardly breathe and only exclamations were the sign of our complete satisfaction, as we came together. It was her third time and I was happy to come now, elated in my climax to burst into her satisfaction…

Sated, she clasped me and then reclined. "I love you…" She fell asleep. I followed her. One thing still crossed my mind. I wanted to lock her bedroom door before I fell asleep. I cuddled close to her and sweet slumber took me into its paradisiacal whorl. There was still quaintness when we woke, she touched me immediately, wanting more. She had her way exciting me. She loved to straddle me and ride with such swift up and down motions, letting herself drop to the base of my cock every now and then. She had turned into the active partner.

Gosh Joan, you fuck sweetly!" I pushed the words in a mix of whisper and short breath. She smiled. "Ah, Zorky, you make me do these things. How good, how wholesome!"

"Joan, I'm free from jealousy and the pain of love at present, you have unbridled my desires for you, I had buried in me for years. I am surprised and happy."

"So am I," she said, "and I want to fuck you now. Stop talking, but tell me lewd words, so I could work up faster to a climax. I want to come again."

"Fuck me Joan, ride ma faster, slow again and move to leave my crown in your pussy, while you start downwards and increase the speed... Harder Joan, be a hard-fucking cunt! Yes, of good, so good my cock sucking sweetheart, let me bite your nipples when you come. For now I'll twist them with my fingers..."

"Pull them, pull them," she cried, oh Jesus, I'm coming soon." That did it to her. Touching her clit triggered this height and arching backwards she catapulted into another climax. "AH – ahh – Zorky, I love you, my lust, I want to come now... ahhh!"

Joan could not stop being excited. And turn my excitement on to match hers. But as usual, I had trained to let her peak first and then as she was flooding me with her excessive body juices, she was always concerned with my peaking. I asked her to turn now slowly, not to completely disconnect. I had to find another sweet spot to chafe my phallus against her soul, inside her vagina. I found it all of a sudden and then it came naturally: Her soul that clasped me and rubbed me into a height of unforeseen sweetness, and yet another time I thought, I couldn't reach another climax in my late stage of life.

"Yes!" I shouted, "yes, I come Joan, you lewd fuck, I come! Ahh! Sweet and lasciviously you place your Venus of Knidos-back toward me, bums stretched-out and all. I bite you," I intonated and clasped her breast with one hand, make her sense my agony. She gasped with me another time and swallowed hard as I came with a strong spray into her. "AHH! Ohh! Sweet fucking Zorky."

All was gone all of a sudden and we still could not leave this magical time together slip away. The best fornication we ever had. I told Joan that this was the case away from the threat of the castle.

"Come, take your best dress and your private belonging and let's leave.

"I can't," she said, "he'll murder sexually provocative Carol-Lee in his rage. "

"Then give me the magical key I've earned and I will take you and Carol-Lee away from the old blaster.

"No way!" Carol-Lee burst into Joan's bedroom.

"Can't you ever knock?" Joan reprimanded her, covering her naked body with the light-blue linen.

"I am happy you fucked, and now he has to pay Zorky his share in the firm, as is the law, otherwise I openly declare him a cuckold and an abuser of his daughters." She stopped and changed her aggressive stance to continue: He could not bear such publicly known shame, but he's finished anyway. His business being investigated, his property soon to be used as a base for the terrorising 'Green Brigades', his brain damaged, I will make an end to his sexual molestations." Her body moves simulated sexual intercourse. "Enough is enough! I will blow the castle up. You two flee and I'll join you soon. I have been well trained in the usage of explosives by my friend Hassim, online."

"No," I said, "Carol, you are in grave danger. He has his bloodhounds around him and they are loose, looting and you know what they will do to a sexy woman like you?" She looked seriously into my eyes.

"You are concerned about me and love me, I can sense that." She came close, placed her hands around me and kissed me. "Thank you Zorky, but I can take care of myself. I had to learn it the hard way. I slip into my battle gear and darken my exposed skin against glare. I can handle them, don't worry. Finally a bomb on all finishing the menace, will be a relief for everybody. It's him or us; I know his final plans." Carol-Lee hugged her Mom and kissed her cheeks. I didn't know Carol could be so sweet. This aspect she'd inherited from Joan. Then she hugged me closely pressing herself onto me. "I love you both," she said emotionally charged. "I want to sleep with you too," she said and started to kiss me. "Before I die..." she said and paused with a tear in her eye. She took my hand placing it on her pussy, and as I stirred her into an arousal, she started to strip me. My pants slid down, my cock was hardening as she went down to accept it between her lips. Joan was kissing me, wanting to share. We landed up in her bed. "My God, I'll die!" I gasped, sensing an unexpected height that would kill me.

"I'll die," I pressed the words between my teeth. Two of my favourite women loving me at the same time. "This is my end, Carol," I whispered and she smiled. I had not seen her smiling in love before. She slipped me a pill and I swallowed it. "Now," she said, "you'll be in your paradisiacal lust, trust me." She slipped her tongue between my parted lips, as if she would chase the sweet pill. In time I felt neither the soreness of my body, nor the overexcitement of sex. I felt with Joan. However, I enjoyed Carol-Lee riding me with her pussy's sucking noises and she initiated what Joan continued, as they took sides. I felt vigorous and on top of the world. It was a long session of excitements and cries by the women. I floated in between a soft bed and the skies. It must have been a good hour that they had their sated climaxes on me, and I was still hard. Then, all I know, Carol was turning and riding me with her back to me, while Joan sat on my face and I tasted her juices, my thirsty mouth sucked in greedily. After that I fell asleep, but sexual overexcitement stirred me half-awake at times. "I gave you Cialis, it works like a dream on you," Carol whispered into my ear lying next to me. "I will make you come, even Mom could learn a thing or two from me," and she started licking my ear that made me moan with pleasure, as I woke up again. Carol spread-out on me, and she chafed my body with her moves, sliding with her swollen lips all over me, kissing me, fellating me close to a height, she artfully avoided to bring to an end. My heart was bursting. "I cannot take anymore," I told her, "it's enough, Carol, I'm not seventeen!" But my words would not come out audibly enough.

"I love you Zarky, indeed, you are a wonderful fuck! Carol whispered and she had her back on my crown enticing me with her sphincter muscle. I kissed Joan, who was next to me, seemingly content and relaxed, as Carol-Lee was her loving daughter who changed her entirely into a quiet, pleasure-giving person. The moment she let me enter her and as I touched my sphincter at the same time, I was on the edge to come – "Uhh! Ahh!"

"You love this Zarky, I knew…OH, I'll come myself, ohhh…She increased her sliding movements.

Suddenly he charged along the passage roaring like a wounded lion. Carol-Lee got up annoyed, looking serious. Immediately she slipped into her battle dress, all black, changing instantly into an Amazon. She rushed-out of the room to deviate his approach. "Lock the door, Zarky!" She was gone.

"Where are the fornicators?" The wild cries of a madman hollered through the passage like thunder.

"I have to go and get the cars ready for shipment to the continent," Carol shouted back.

"Then go!" She returned her answers in the same high-pitched tone, and then started to call him lewd names. "Go and fuck your cars, she added.

Joan in her fright had dressed in a hurry into her good clothes, took the box with her jewellery and emptied her personal wall safe in a hurry. She stuffed all into her large bag and placed the remainder of her things into a black rucksack. Then she placed more heavy items into it and she asked me to carry it for her. "Hurry Zarky, and come close behind me." She rushed forward having dressed with her lightweight athletic shoes, I followed behind her, at first with difficulties. "There," she said, "take the key." I turned it in the lock on the floor. The set-in door gave way and the spring opened a trapdoor. We had just slipped below ground onto a landing, as I heard Bull-man burst the door to Joan's bedroom. He shouted, cajoled, ripped at the linen of her bed, shouting more and already beyond control in a sick rage. I asked Joan to rush toward the exit and wait there for me. I heard Carol-Lee's cries "Wait Zarky, wait for me!" Joan turned. "You love her?" She asked looking seriously.

"I don't know," I replied, "just now I want to help her to escape the madman. I love you both!" I said, but Joan was already gone. Just as I intended to close and lock the trapdoor, Carol-Lee appeared just in time. "Wait, please, wait, Zarky, Take me in!" I held the door up and she jumped into my hands, fast as a weasel sliding down along me. I held her tight, she was breathing heavily. I kissed her and she relaxed.

"OK, Zarky love, thank you, now lock the trapdoor." I did it immediately, twice, then I pocketed the key. "Oh gosh," she said pressing close to me in the confines of the escape shaft, "you are aroused and I cannot even go down on you here!" We laughed. I let her slip down towards the landing, where Joan had landed first. "Wait Carol, let me go first, it's tricky here and I have a torch." I slid down on her body and her pants slipped down exposing her triangle of pubic hair. I could feel the moisture at my lips, kissing her pussy. My tongue slipped out to caress her. She became wet. As I closed my hands around her bums, I could sense her excitement to peak soon. My little finger played around her anal opening that tightened as I licked her. Touching her clit made her shudder. I held her fast as she buried her palms into my hair, clasping it with her closed fists. She came and my whole face was wet with her warm juices – I felt an uncontrollable urge to take Carol-Lee. I joined her at the landing and pulled her pants down. I lifted her up, loosened my belt and slid my jeans down. Then Carol would slide onto my penis, her hands placed against the rough plastered wall of the escape passage. "We don't have much time," she whispered – ah – oh Zarky love – hurry up – no, well we'll die together if we do not escape soon – oh – how wonderful. Oh – I have never loved like this before – Ahh! She was so wet and I was finding my spot to push into her. This time I was ready. "I come, Carol – Oh! Sweet Lee..." She cried out.

We hurried up and descended the passage. Carol pulled me along. I had an emotional collapse, bit did not tell her. Suddenly she changed her facial expression.

"I have to get him, I feel strong now."

"I'll come with you."

"No," she said, "give me the key. I love you," she said and disappeared. While we made love she told me her idea how to kill him. She had shown me her scar. I had noticed before, but had forgotten to ask her about. It was him, she said. Once he misused me and fucked me in my sleep. As I kicked his balls, he stuck the silver letter-opener I got from Hassim in Egypt towards me, but missed to drive it into my belly. "Let me kiss your scar," I said. As I hurried down the sloping passage, I saw her beautiful body laid out and I wanted her, kissing her thigh, where the thin scar was visible. It lead me invariable to her pubic hair. She had reacted by spreading her legs apart as my lips touched the moistness of her vulva. I enjoyed Carol-Lee, as she was wet instantly, a sensual woman who loved to love well. She moaned and let the waves of lust wash over her with the movements of my tongue. Then she took turns on me.

We matched, even Joan had noticed. Women have a fine sensory perception. She had a tear in the corner of her eye. "Go now," she had said, "I will be all right, take care of Mom. I'll send you a message." I checked her mobile phone number. I left, cried, and ran. There wasn't time left. It was anger against the monster, the protective role and my responsibility, and my bursting love for Carol. The danger she was in and the love I was able to give her as a back-up for her brave act, filled me with an arousal, just as I reached the exit and Joan. I was a fortunate man, rich, and filled with love. "I hope Carol knows what to do," I said to Joan as I kissed her. She was warm and receptive.

Carol-Lee rushed off to her secret chambers, once she had emerged from the trapdoor, in the walk-in cupboard of Joan's room. It was located at the end of the work-shops, where Bluebeard had his vintage cars fixed, altered, and the new ownership numbers stamped in to legalize the stolen property as his. She worked above the shop and could watch the ongoing through a gap in the wooden ceiling. His valet had brought him down in a wheelchair and he demanded to be seated in his favourite new model of a Jaguar XP. He loved especially Jaguar cars as his personal treat. While she observed him, her heart went out to Zarky. What an impromptu lover he was. His instant arousals and his great strength, as she was sliding along the rough wall with her palms stretched out, and her lower body arched into his standing position. What an excellent fuck! It gave her strength and determination to kill Bluebeard now. He was nuts about his type of car the team had to bring them in a dozen times. She did not know where they all came from. This one here was a special custom-made edition. That's what he was so obsessed with. A piece of art, he had uttered. Maybe he collected them from all over the Dark Continent, beyond the borders that lay beyond the mountains of the peninsula. For sure, she would soon know, as she had set the explosives into his car and at the castle's major structural points, which supported the stonework. Timing! Timing, she said to herself and her mind worked feverishly to complete the rigging of the areas he usually stayed in. Now is the time to do it, now, before he goes to rest. She hurried away on cat-paws to plant the explosive devices. Then, as he took his nap, she could rig-up the surrounding areas of his bedrooms. She lined the devices into the ceiling spaces and then used the air-conditioning shafts. Then she planted the bombs into the series of cupboards, wherever the usage was poor. All completed, she felt her adrenalin pumping. Carol took deep breaths. Just as Hassim, the city bomber had taught her. He enjoyed most of all, bombing virtual cities, he had first built. They had met and fallen in love over their hobbies. This Internet-love kept her going for all those years, after the sleep-rape of her father. Mary had told her that he was perhaps her stepfather, as he was away during the war, when Joan had become pregnant. Just to soothe her guilt and bad feelings. It was though not effective with her, she had turned into a sexual insulting tornedo. Hassim, her soulmate had trained her the way, he was once trained by the radical arm of the revolutionary forces in his country. His teacher, a beautiful Amazon woman, was killed in one of the raids. She had slept with him the night before, falling in love with him, missing a split-second concentration. Since then he had abandoned the idea of becoming a terrorist, and he stuck to teach computer games and the building of websites. That's where he met Carol-Lee, who was upset and prepared to kill her father. Soul-mates – he called the state of their liaison, masturbation – she called it. Now she had to collect all the wires joining them to the central detonators. She had self-fabricated old-fashioned bombs, she wanted to blast, besides ones, where she could trigger a detonator with the aid of her cellular phone signals, as on his car. She waited for another thirty seconds to check the standby mode of her installation. It checked-out fine.

The descend to Joan's bedroom was through the trapdoors in the ceiling and the place of her walk-in cupboard, where she arrived with a bundle of cables, she connected to the detonator device she placed carefully into the ceiling, next to the trapdoor. Then she closed all. Opening the trapdoor to the escape passage with the key Zarky had given her, she descended into the shaft. She stood there for a moment, while the door shut close and before she switched on her mini-powered torch, thinking of Zarky, as he had slid down on her and took her hippants down kissing her belly. She could feel his tongue working its trail along her belly onto her thighs, and as she desired it, into her vulva. He had already brought her to an instant height.

"I love you Zarky," she said aloud as she descended the steel steps to the landing that lead to the secret escape passage. The door at the end of the passage was slightly ajar. Zarky had left it for her, she thought, being yet cautious approaching it. There – a shadow. She froze, slowly reached for her handgun at her belt and pointed the laser aim towards the dark figure next to the doorframe. Intuitively she pressed the trigger. The silencer had belted a few times and there was a thud, as if somebody had fallen. In the beam of her light she saw the face of one of Bluebeard's body guards. He was dead. She peeked through the escape door. There was no sign of anybody else. I hope Zarky and Joan are safe, she said to herself, as she ran in a zigzag fashion towards the cops of birch trees. She collapsed on the ground pressing all the buttons... Darn! Nothing happened. Suddenly she recalled that she had forgotten the prefix-code. What is it? The same as my personal banking code, she heard her inside voice activated. OK. The four numbers came to her. Damned. She usually knew the figures instantly. She loaded it into her phone. As she finished dialling progressing further into the nearby woods, the first explosion thundered. A steep flame flared into the sky from the centre of the castle taking shards of debris with it, some falling around thirty metres from her position. As she ran deeper into the woods, the staggered explosions came one after the other. She knew that she had done a good job and Bluebeard would be dead. The car! She thought of the Jag. He must have known that she had rigged the castle; someone had raised suspicion, that's why he had sent his bodyguard, who would be intercepting anyone fleeing from the secret passage. Zarky must have left the door ajar, to aide her escape, but the guard had slipped into the cool shadow to remain undetected. Darned. Lucky me. What about them? Well, as nobody is around they must have escaped with the Blaster. She pushed herself flat to the ground behind a huge beach tree. Then she waited. A piece of wood fell through the trees, not far from her. His bed, she thought, now he is dead. She got up and walked, her knees were shaking. Deeper in the woods, she regained her fast and vigorous gait. Then she was running along a trodden path until she was out of breath. Her chest hurt. She stopped to listen. Nothing, not a sound, but soft splashes of a waterfall. She desired a refreshing dip. It was time to wash off her black stripes of paint. Dipping into the cool water she gasped, coming up for air. She finished washing and put her jeans on her wet body. There was a noise in the underground and she grabbed her handgun pointing towards it. Then a net covered her instantly and she was caught. "We don't want to harm you," a female voice said. Carol clasped her hands in front of her breasts as she was let free by some dark-clothed men, their faces hidden behind baklavas. The woman pulled her baklava off to reveal her golden-blond short cropped hair and her smile on her beautiful lips.

"We'll leave you alone if you help us. We know you blew up Bluebeard's castle."

"Damned!" Carol cried, "I forgot!" She took her phone and pressed number seven. "Ah! Just in time," she said.

"Aha," the blond woman said to her. "Did you kill him?"

"I hope so," Carol replied. "Now what do you do next?"

"We need an explosives expert." The blond woman smiled.

*

Poinciana

He went to the gym, as part of his weekly routine. Most of the time he made it every second day to the bright and airy hall, if business accommodated his one-hourly time off. Work came first, but at times he coughed at work, especially if clients became obsessive or impossible, insatiable with changing their minds, often they just wished to satisfy one of their whims.

He had to switch his mobile phone to receive messages and then he drove home, his blood-pressure had been pushed up, as he could feel the pulsations in his temples. He did not bother to take a reading, as his doctor had recommended, but having changed into comfortable clothes he aimed for the kitchen. Preparing a simple but well-seasoned meal sedated his temper and soothed his upset inner life. Since the death of his soulmate he could not find peace easily. But there were some friends he corresponded with and some were more accessible than others. One person at a time responded to his communicative efforts.

The tomatoes simmered in the cast iron pot. He added garlic and oregano, his favourite herb. Some minutes later he blended some capers to the boiling tomatoes, then sprinkled some Turmeric spice across. The smell of mingling herbs and garlic with the sweet tomatoes wafted through the air, heaven-like perfume for him. He thirsted for a beer, opened the high-tech fridge and retrieved a cooled bottle of Pilsner light from the door shelf. Cooled at eleven degrees Celsius, he thought of being the right temperature for that brew. His taste buds already anticipating the first sip, were on high alert. He opened the bottle. As he poured its content carefully into a tulip-shaped glass, he held it slightly tilted to avoid over-foaming. As the foam reached the height of an inch, he stopped and placed the glass to his lips. MH! The first sip was delicious.

Wholesome. He felt already better, and his blood-pressure had returned to normal. The water in the spaghetti-pot had still to be boiled.

In the meantime he returned to the lounge taking his beer along. He sat down in his favourite chair, in the corner of the room, took a magazine from the low table and opened a marked spot. He glanced over an article about New York City that interested him. How fascinating a place, he thought, always preparing to visit one day. Time's up, he said aloud, having reinforced his background research about this city, which had given him the background for the two love-birds, who met on the observation deck of the ESB – as Americans use acronyms – the Empire State Building. He noticed that the water was boiling. He rose and mumbled: NYC, and ESB, wondering if every American used these in their daily talks, while he took a few steps into the compact kitchen.

He placed the spaghetti into the boiling water. Fifteen minutes, he made a mental note, as they were the thicker kind. He stirred the sauce on the low flame and added some oats to thicken the sauce. He checked his watch, while he stepped back into the living room taking up his reading about the ESB. He couldn't recall the names of the architects, but he remembered the skyscraper to be an Art-Deco building of the thirties. For forty years it rained as the tallest building on earth. He repeated the names, he found in the article: Shrieve, Lamb and Harmon. His friend had asked him some time ago about that and he could only name him the second of the three partners, as a colleague of his had the same name.

Time was up. He switched the boiling water off and tasted the spaghetti. Cooked through a bit more than al-dente, as he usually preferred it, he replaced the perforated lid, took two kitchen gloves and locking the lid of the cover with the handles, emptied the water through the sieve, tilting the pot into the sink. Then, replacing the pot on the stove, he selected a white plate, calling his spouse to bring her plate. With the forked server he placed a portion of spaghetti on her plate, just as she preferred it, adding sauce on top of it.

At the dining table, she had set before, she added parmesan cheese to both of their plates, then she fell immediately over her food, eating like a bird taking small bits on her fork. While he twisted his fork around bigger portions of spaghetti, as he had learned to eat this dish in Italy, chewing mouthfuls with gusto. He finished fast. An inner unrest made him chew his food speedier and swallow faster than she did hers. Finished, he apologized and got up from the table to take his empty plate to the sink.

"It tastes delicious, John," she mumbled. He hurried through the back door across the terrace and down two steps to the grassed area in front of his study. Unlocking the safety door he entered his domain.

He sat down in his adjustable armchair. The world he entered let him forget the other world he was fleeing from. In the last five years he had created his world of magical design, poetry, painting, and writing. This was the place where he felt at home. At last at ease, something inside him struggled to come to the fore. He drew a picture for a while and then he continued to finish some drafting work for a client's domicile. After that he paused and wished to reward himself with a few hours of typing up his latest conceptualized poems into his PC. He thought of Imis, put his head down and dedicated her a poem. He recalled immediately her radiating dusky eyes that had a strong magnetic effect on him, turning his knees to soft tissue. He wished to touch her lips, crafted like a Classical sculpture's face, with his fingertips first, before following with his lips. He desired her.

Placing a disc into the CD player of his personal computer he listened to the Jarrett trio. Keith's piano virtuosity catapulted him into another world. Now he could start falling into his artistic groove, the prelude to enter the caverns of creativity. At one stage he thought of succumbing to madness. It was his intense love of a woman who had made-up her mind to seduce him. She had set a trap he was falling into, being enticed by her to take the initiative to seduce her first. She made him think of being such a Romeo. Ha! She had dialled his telephone number and then, as he showed interest in her, she cut the line. As she disappeared from his life, after love's short bouts of orgasm – swallowed up by a giant whale of void – he felt floating on his raft of erotic survival on a roughed-up sea of dark emotions. The raft that carried his soul into nowhere, he called: 'The ship of fools'.

It took him on an odyssey to the North Sea, where he was thrown by a storm onto a beach. Someone found him and shook his shoulder. He noticed her gentle touch and her dusky eyes first, then her smile. She spoke with a foreign accent and his mind smitten by her appearance, he just gazed at her. When he recovered from his pleasant awakening, she handed him his clothes, cleaned and dry. She fed him and played for him some music from her native eastern lands and she spoke: "Just friends, I'm not running after men."

"OK," he said, "I'm not running after women, I pursue them." She laughed. He liked her immediately. The music came through his earphones, he preferred to speakers. They had a higher quality of sound and he could notice all refinements. It was a blues-theme, exhilaratingly beautiful. Indeed it was great. He recalled the Duke's tune: *A Prelude to a Kiss.* Did he guess the title?

He wrote with regained fervour. All of a sudden she appeared on his screen, the beautiful photograph sent by electronic mail. Ah! Imis! She appeared as a goddess to him, somebody extraordinary with a set of tremendous bodylines, representing Aphrodite to him. Besides a beautiful creature, she oozed intelligence and talents, at times writing poetry, but she hesitated of making regular use of them. She kept a low profile preferring secrecy and at most of her meetings she acted taciturn.

He gazed at her picture: Imis with eyes closed, caressed by her dog, her beloved Benjie – or so he recalled she had once called him – as she had asked him to meet her. The Scottish sheep dog had been attached to her with his vivid behaviour. Could a dog be as much part of her as she appeared to be part of it?

He thought of her as a woman with the head of a dog, as depicted in the hierarchy of Egyptian Gods. Or did it suit the dog to have a human appearance as its body? Is it the animal we want to be around us physically who had torn itself from our innermost and materialized? We all carry an animal in us. Our sun signs relate mostly to the animal world. His mind stirred into the world of mythology and he gazed at the stars above him, as he stepped outside his study. Great to breathe fresh air like this, he thought. Then he stepped back into his study again.

He sat down again placing his headphones on his ears. He played Keith Jarrett again. The second CD was affecting his senses so much that he became frenzied listening to *Poinciana,* the music he had heard in the pub in Kew, where he sat with her sharing a talk, smiles, and a drink. The outside light had faded into twilight, he loved at this location. The water on the low-flowing Thames was rippled and the sun's dwindling rays made it glisten in a silvery and golden flicker with orange flares in between. Lights and water made love. Perhaps the stained window of deep colours transferred his feelings to her. The smoothness of her skin spread angelically over her warm and contagious smile. Like a 'Persian cat', he thought, no, 'like a peacock's colours projected onto a Persian cat.

He knew then that he loved her, but how much time would it take to be with her again? He could realize his dreams in writing, as they became words he wrote down on the white sheets of paper that lay in abeyance strewn all across his desk, heaped-up, waiting for his inspiration that would take them and turn rapacious with his erotic text. And if he became drawn into the whorl of the creative process, he would transfer the written words into a painting.

Her picture stirred in him feelings of longing for her physical presence and the romance of a late afternoon river walk below the low covers of stringing willow trees, where he could at intervals steal a kiss from her, even only for a start of an unusual romantic story that had been waiting for him to be experienced, felt, and written, waiting for him to pick-up the flowers, abandoned by someone whose date did not turn-up, left behind in anger, and he could enhance her feelings towards him with these abandoned pink roses, part of an innocent and a young blossoming life. He would refresh them with cold water and keep the delicate roses alive in a basin, with their stems having a good soak, until it was time to meeting Imis again.

This was the music's interpretation he pitched against his feelings: *Poinciana*. Exactly! Such a great treat of a CD he had bought in an unknown shop on intuition, to paint the romantic setting for his creative writings. That's when she appeared and he couldn't complete her picture without these imaginary sounds. She still remained mute to him and at an arms-length distance. Now, as he could complete her colourful picture, he had found her again in good vibrations. He wrote her a letter and danced.

*

The Chafing

Once she had surprised him. Young and lithe, she extolled vitality and speed. He loved to see her excel in anything she did. It gave him a thrill and pulled his inner stirrings to excel in something she did appreciate as well. In group-sport she was always among the best, up in front of the crowd that followed her, a born leader. She loved a rough game, enjoying the thrill of speed and tenacity of basketball, she advanced to the game of women-rugby.

"Where do you get thirty women at a time falling over each other and entangle in each other's hair?" She joked and laughed. He adored her, almost as a sacred animal chafing against the hordes as if to dominate them.

When he met her, she was shy but a sensitive teenager, who preferred elderly men, feeling secure with them, as they would view her as a gift from heaven, adoring her beauty and praising her clear mind. They would not pass comments about the handicap of her injured left hand; she had once nearly severed with a set of sharp shears, an incident that left her blemished. She was conscious about her hand and she tried to compensate for it, accelerating herself to a Wonder-Woman figure. He used to console her, never even entering his mind about her handicap. He made her welcome, feel good about herself, and value her inner qualities of honesty and integrity. It all did not matter to him one way or another. It was a natural part of her, and when he saw her she always came close to him. When nobody was around, they kissed. Her full lips stung their sweetness into him, a welcome poison of seduction that shook his body and stirred a sensational burn in his loins. He had to think of a bee sting and the subsequent swelling, the increase of his heartbeat, and the pain that converted pain to pleasure. He never queried why.

She was already as a teen a beautiful girl with long brunette hair that had tinges of copper against the sun, she kept braided in one long piece that fell down to her waist. He followed her in secret as he knew the place where she took her clothes off after a long morning's hunt in the woods, to take a bath in the pristine waters of a spring-fed pond. He had observed her body growth with greater and greater fondness. He desired her. She did her hair after a swim and dried it in the sun. She reminded him of his mother from behind, as he had watched her as a kid doing her hair. He thought about the snow of her breasts all the time, she had eventually noticed, but did not want to make him aware of it, as she enjoyed his eyes on her body, causing her sweet sensations. She wanted him. Once he did mention this to her and she blushed, as if she had been caught by her daddy, swimming in the nude, but it gave her pleasure to be gazed over by a man. As it gave her pleasure to be with him, he teased her lovingly.

In the shadow of his retreat, where she came to eventually, he took her immediately into his arms; she desired to be squeezed hard against him and to be taken by him. He took her blouse off, admiring her breasts and her hardened nipples with dark-pink aureoles. She enjoyed all his kisses on them, his tender yet hungry caressing. He did not go further. She was changing into a young and full-bloodied woman, letting steam off by wrestling with her sisters and the boys from next door, and then chafing her breasts against their bodies. She saw his face thirty-fold at all times. After the games her heated body needed a cool-down. She rushed out and ran to Joe's Place. He wasn't surprised, closed the door after her and took her into his arms. She continued wrestling with him and they landed on his bed.

She took his shirt off, but he did not allow her to take his jeans off. Then she slipped out of her tee-shirt. The cushions of her beautiful breasts suffocated him as she pressed them hard against his face. He let her cool-off, let her chafe and wriggle until she found a way of getting excited , rubbing her pussy against the bulge in his jeans. She came to a height, then another. He caressed her full breasts. She moaned, threw her head back and she bit him into his arms. Then she calmed down. He admired her body and she turned into a cat, he stroked gently.

They talked about her dreams and her fantasies. She wanted to know everything, all at once. He took it slowly, one step at a time. He let her feel this fire within her that started to flash and fade. As soon as he touched her, she wished to have a height, working frantically to get there. She was indeed highly sensual.

For years she came and he kissed her. They had built a tender relationship that went wild with her, but only at the start of every meeting. Joe had powers in him that captured her eventually, and she had what she wanted: Understanding with care on top of sexual fulfilment, at least as far as he wanted it to proceed, never fully pene-trating her. "That's for your future spouse," he said to her.

For years she carried on seeing him, whenever he re-turned from his month-on-end long trips. Indeed, he al-ways enjoyed returning to the undulating green fields, the dark-emerald woods, he thought of being synonymous with her person. She waited for him. She wanted to kiss him, be held and loved. In one moment the wild temper of her pent-up feelings broke free and she caught him in the shower. Wrapping herself around him she chafed herself on his hip-bone until she cried, the warm water gushing down on them. Then she lowered herself, knelt on the floor and started kissing his cock. She wanted him now and there was no escape for him, besides, he wanted her too. A thunderstorm raced outside Joe's Place across the lands and penetrated his chest. He stretched and heaved and gasped. This time she wanted him to suffer the ten-sions she had endured, while he was away. This time she wanted all to turn into the sweetness she expressed with her lips. This time she wanted to swallow him completely.

She came into his life by accident: He, her pet-poet, her new Joe, who followed a vocation, met her one day ex-perimenting with a play, choosing avatars on a program that was offered online. He liked her instantly. She was soft-spoken and had that specific accent that appeared to him exotic and charming, with an edge of intellect he appreciated in a female counterpart. She had brought a girlfriend along, who must have had a few spiked drinks, as she talked about sex casually. It was then that he decided to be with her and not her girlfriend, who wished to express her needs graphically, without even knowing him. His stimulation related to the mind by its use rather than an artificial dulling of it, destroying its natural function that was strange to him, and he couldn't see the sense of it. He offered Elle his friendship and she accepted. They wrote each other, as Elle was always drawn to writing. In her schooldays she had written plays for all school performances. She inspired him to write a story and created a theme for him, or she gave him a prompt. He reacted and sent her the result. She became his natural muse and he started writing an epic poem about the story of an odyssey, as she represented to him the woman he wanted, but she was thousands of miles to the west and he lamented that fact: "We are together adrift." This became his main theme for his poems for her for some time. He amused her, entertained her, read his poems for her, enjoyed listening to her voice, he imagined to fit to the words she sent him all the time. He wished to excel in writing, as she did with her schooling and sporting activities. She had courage; he wondered how it would be if he could meet her at all. Would he love her as much as in this realm of communicative moods?

He practised his writing skills and she encouraged that. They shared their lives in words an in a lively exchange of increasing need for communication. He fell in love with her many times. It as a fondness, a longing inside him. He met her on her request, to be told that she was going to be engaged. They met on her island of their dreams for the last time. She took him on a tour. He pulled her leg and teased her to making love in the bowels of a ship. After all it was a virtual adventure and they did shine! A brilliant pair it seemed. He thought of heroes, like Captain Cook, a dashing Robert Taylor of the Hollywood of his youth, and he wondered who her hero was. He thought of her as a Madonna of the Seas, a peacock of Fantasy Isle, where she took him to introduce him to her friends.

From time on she sailed to the Northern ice: Alaska. She liked the exotic world of eternal iced peaks and permafrost, but she fell ill. He received from her pictures about the beauty of iridescent coloured icebergs, including him as participant in her new environment. She described her impressions, sending him innumerable photographs and pictures of herself. She seemed reasonably happy with her family, but had a recurring homesick feeling for the lands of green hills and emerald forests, at the wild creek where she grew-up, where she still could meet her poet again. He was part of her life. Already, added to the flock of her family of four children, not her own, besides she expected her first child. He felt though that he hadn't lost her to a spouse, or another friend, not anybody. He had gained her rather, gained that part of her soul she kept like a treasure buried deep inside her being, nobody could access but him, her poet, the one admiring her from the start of her adult life. She was fond of him and on and off in love with him, thinking of him as her new Joe.

He never changed, remaining a virile elderly man she was attracted to. She encouraged him to write her some stories, tell her his fantasies that might be about her. As soon as she read one of his poems, or his stories, she loved him through these verses and prose, immediately spurring on her own creative angle she had forgotten about. It had been a realm they had built together over these years, a place she could escape to in times of personal troubles or difficulties; then at times to find only pleasure. It was her way of coping with life, drawing new energy from it and from him. Still having a good number of years left, he was often acknowledging the distant twilight of his life drawing closer. She loved him this way and he responded to her love, often placing herself into the palms of his hands. It could be intense at a given moment and become real in the act of communication. As soon as he wanted to hold her, love her, and cry-out with her together, the pictorial atmosphere disappeared. Gone like a spook, as a breeze, she left behind her scent, her image, and her face as an imprint on his body, and he craved for her for some time, imagining how her body still felt on his own, that scene he could only see on his monitor enlarged as big as possible.

Their correspondence though was continual and reasonably regular, albeit their desires shot off in different directions and turned their glow on to others. By good luck both had fine spouses they could turn to as their friends. In love they were fortunate, always enticing and often enticed by someone pleasant. Many waited around to have a good time, but then it happened to be people who couldn't live up to the high expectations placed on them, and finally most turned out to be quite disappointing.

Joe and Elle, the unusual togetherness continued. There was never the query about age difference in their minds. It was something unimportant and did not count on their scale of deeper friendship.

One day he found her in her new home, she had rented from Joe, the man, who was once in her life the elder, gentler being, who taught her tenderness within her sentimental education. She visited again, now a Diana of the forest and hunt, who had her bow and arrow replaced with a gun. Her dog at her side, she excelled as a crack shot. Her dress was as short and revealing as the one of Classical goddesses. Was it then not Joe, the poet, she had revisited all her life, Joe, the man with loving arms and gentle demeanours, who taught her about the sweeter things in life? Could he not unfold all the pleasurable layers buried in her chest and bring them to life at an instant? He was her loving guide throughout these secret meetings, where she would immerse with him unbridled into the subtleties of love

While she prepared for a life as a professional healer, her friend, Joe, the poet, travelled the lands at the Mediterranean Sea, searching for her twin-sister. She had told him about her being in trouble and he intended to find her. He continued writing poems for Elle having great longing for her, calling her his personal healer. Having still a gashing wound from love, he was about to lose his limbs and even his mind. He couldn't find her twin-sister.

He summoned Elle and she came immediately. He was bleeding to death and hands-on trying to save his life. She had experience being highly erotic and transferring her emotions to him. Joe loved to look at her and hear her gasps. He asked her often to stand model for him, as he wanted to draw her at such moments. Joe was a full-bloodied artist. He craved for her shapely bodylines, especially her full and beautiful breasts. He drew her lovingly, stroking her shapes with his pencil movements, recreating her every time.

Finally, after all these years she was here, in the nude in front of him. He touched her, kissed her, and in his ritual of adoration he loved her and fell into her body. She had enticed him with a lover's sixth sense to bring him to the boil. Then he started to heal from the wounds of a love that had been a matter of life and death. His woman he had loved had been abducted, taken from him in the cruellest way. She had been declared to be terminally ill out of the blue and decided to keep the bad news from him. It did not fit into the greater picture of love she had painted for him all this time, and he fell into this illusionary landscape, a real island, a real love, but then there was a void just behind it, the greatest abyss of his life to date: Death. She disappeared. A ghost.

Her part in him died the same way as the fading of her image. He suffered, his conscious mind confused, but still fighting the great deception by fate.

"Elle," he cried out with a hoarse voice, "Elle, help me!" That was all he was able to mutter. She took him to her generous bosom and caressed him, fed him like a baby, suckling him. He was suddenly tiny, cuddled-up to his mother, receiving all her love and nourishment.

Elle was the lover, the woman he desired, the cushion of her beautiful breasts was his home. He recovered, he wanted all of her, but she would teach him touches of fingers and stroking of hands, the delicate use of the face, eyes, nose, lips and tongue. This was the heaven he had asked for. "You Elle and your fingers, your pursed sweet lips bee-stinging me!"

He travelled a lot, couldn't find his peace, even if he squandered half of his inherited fortune to find her again. There are moments of great joy, when he detects a new island, a new woman who reminds him of her. He could sense her presence, talking through this woman's voice to him. He falls in love with her and she responds. A high-pitched voice will change the illusion. His mind still deceived, will pull back, as if he'll avoid to be bitten by a snake, crossing bare-footed a thick-grassy mound.

Would Elle come and sing and tell her stories he had induced in her? Will she make the trees listen, the rocks, appeal to their hearts and make them cry? Would she enter the dark void of the underworld and tell her heart-gripping stories he had given her? Stories about the powers of life and death? Will she save him from the state of remaining at the gate of a 'Duat' – the mysterious in-between-of-worlds? Would she be a strong, good woman and not turn until they reached the line to cross into the upper world of light, so he could live again and share all innocent moments of deep pleasure with her?

She's on the way to him now and soon she'll travel to the end of the world to seek him. A great life would begin. He could take after her maiden landing, to see with him together places of great sense, join the spirit of truth through history and fly together in love and joy. He could. He has to stay patient, patience he has learned all those years from his chafing with lust and love, life and death.

*

The Electric Rainbow Slide

This is 'Joburg'," she said and took my hand. Her big blue-green eyes shone in layers like the lights outside, signalling promising messages like a lit-up sky, taking me unawares. Her fine, long fingers curled around my stubby writing hand. Her presence stirred me, but most of all her full breasts that touched me now and then, as she came close to me. She smiled then, projecting spiteful curls on her lips, stating some intelligent remarks that sparkled with mental brilliance. She appeared sharp and alert, oiled like a new Ferrari engine, placing her best foot forward, then she opened the silver clasp that held her hair together. It fell to her shoulders and beyond, a waterfall of dark-brunette waves. Then she threw her head back and laughed, changing suddenly her mocking remarks into soft cooing. Like birds we danced in an initial play of our pent-up feelings. I held her in my arms as the music started to play *Libertango,* her svelte body moved like a sleek sculpture, her legs slipped from her jeans revealing a red body stocking. All eyes on her slender feet, as she moved one leg – she emerged in a winding around my waist. I held her by her thigh; her passionate movement let me touch her below it as she moved. In this passionate dance expressions our hearts met, entwined, dissolved and parted, to come close again, mingling for a moment and to rejoice with an inner cry together. Sadness and joy were breathing together tonight, as always. How come we do this song and dance? The question remained unanswered. Back in her jeans and her soft sweater again, she calls. "Come with me," and she stepped aside, passed one woman who was keen to draw attraction to herself, impulsive in her cries with derogatory remarks against the lecturing guest writer from the British Isles.

"You must give her a chance to talk," a voice silenced the heckler, "however conservative she ever appears."

"What is your name?" The heckler-woman said, "Why don't you entertain us with your erotic dance?

"Mara," she replied, "and the erotic dance is called Tango. Do you know how to do it?"

"I've heard of it," I said.

"Kiss me," she said, as my mouth dropped open. "Zed, come now!" She took my hand again. I felt ashamed, I said to her that I had long forgotten by now, but once I desired to hear all these love words. I held her tighter and then bent her slowly backward. Then I kissed her with an intensity that made her shiver with pleasure. Concentrating to transfer my feelings I placed into this kiss, one hand on her back, the other one sliding down on her spine with total dedication. "My …like Rodin…" she gasped.

"Enough, enough for that. Take me up again," she said,"now to the second act," she gasped again: "We came here together, two people in love." Standing next to me she placed her hand around my waist. She shouted "Now!" Suddenly we changed into a different couple. Mara shouted: "Poets, well prepared, well on their way. Take us great Zan, take us!"

The Windows on top of this musical tower to Burg, sounded strange to him changing into a soft white cloud that floated on the velvet of the night-sky. Light and independent the comfortable lounge changed shape to a bus a train, and into a racing car next, driving us dilly with its own crazed will at a whim. Mara said "Zetty, take it easy". Our thoughts must have crossed continually in opposite directions. "You may go through to any place you wish," a voice sounded, "Use all possibilities of power-thought!"

"Mandela Square," he said and the sculpture turned into the human shape of a Michelangelo figure, and settled above the famous Square. "This is not Mandela Square," he said, "all's light blue."

"Symbol for peace," Mara said. Fascinating how the big man, appearing light-blue, moved to the shuffle that carried his name; happiness expressed for a better future. "Let's shuffle with him," he said and they danced to

'Quaito'-music. How human and exciting! This is fun, how different the city appears through all this tonight.

"What's next? She said.

"You choose Mara."

"Well, I'd like to go to Gandhi Square," she uttered and waited for the Michelangelo-shape to change and turn into an Indian elephant. It took them through the clear night air on his well-decorated back with comfortable seats, firstly downtown as a myriad of light clusters came closer towards them. Their faces became dark-blue and crimson coloured. He had to laugh, the elephant trumpeted with sheer exuberance. He followed their wishes instantly, following site for site, Square for Square, then they landed with a Ford Model T in front of them. 'City Hall' the crimson letters said on the pristine white façade. "A famous landmark," Mara whispered. Seated in the magical Ford T, the car took them for a spin around the Square and the streets surrounding it, passed some vagrants in colourful feathered dresses and groups of late night onlookers, who were celebrating. They all gathered in front of a giant screen showing 'The Magic Flute', as a modern transferred version of a surrealist artist. The night birds applauded and popped the corks of champagne bottles. The screen turned into a slide-show: A giant peacock, bull-bulls gathering on the back of rhinos, flamingos danced around in the Square's huge instantly flooded lake. The African bush with lions, leopards, cheetahs, giraffes, elephants. The Big Five, a huge advert announced the trip to the bush as sensation of a life time. Hyenas appeared cracking the empty champagne bottles...

"I'm afraid Zetty," she said and placed her arm into his.

"Don't be, Mara," he replied, "come closer." The only way he could be closer to her, since he met her six months back, when circumstances were changing for him, like for many people. He had met her at a writers meeting. Her self-assured voice triumphed. She appeared to him as an established novelist, although she thought of herself as a budding amateur. A great talent, he concluded for himself, with genial strokes of excellence in an inspired style of writing. Now she didn't write. "What's wrong with you, Mara? He said aloud, "why did you stop writing?"

"I need to gather more experience," she said.

"Nonsense," he said, holding her tight and her breathing became faster. He could feel her pointed breasts touching him as she breathed in.

"I am aroused," he said, "write about that!"

"No. Let's go to the Central Station," she announced and he frowned. "The place is desolate and in need of being cleaned-up, to be restored for a new lease on its life," he said. Thinking of a coach, one appeared. "Hah!" he laughed, "just in good time! Take us to a train coach."

The amber lighting made it a strange place to spend time there, as they arrived in a railway coach pulled by a steam engine. The white steam coloured the amber light and the atmosphere turned eerie.

"Let's sit here on a bench, smoke a cigarette I received as a present from a fellow poet." He lit the hand-made cigarette for her. The scent of sweet treacle wafted into his nose. "It smells like a joint," he remarked.

"It's hand-made in Bombay," she said and took another drag she kept-in for some time, then exhaled, blowing rings that took on the amber colour of the space. People passed by like shadows on a stage.

"I didn't know you smoked," he said and she took his hand. "Have a drag," she said and cure your prejudices." She smiled as she stuck the cigarette between his fingers. He then took a long drag. It tasted sweet and made his head immediately feel light. "Mhh, it's special," he said, "we'll get high." He handed her the joint. "Not that much," she replied, dragging on it greedily and her eyes began express a wild look. He stared at her.

"You frighten me," he said, "are you sure it will not hurt you? This stuff has an effect like alcohol. It's awesome!"

"Let's go to Joubert Park, the Art museum," he said. She gave her cigarette to a begging youngster and they took off to the skies in a modified monstrous bird from a

Norman Catherine painting. The new destination looked great from above.

"You normally do not see this view in the midst of the city's street ravines." He said forlorn.

"It must be this cigarette from Bombay," she giggled, "it has expanded our minds." He smiled and felt an unusual serenity enveloping him as he kissed her.

*

The Spirit of the Flame Tree

On a recent trip to a forlorn beach, Zeno arrived on a winding road along the south-eastern beaches of Crete. Taking the left branch of the road that followed east of Ierapetra, he felt suddenly tired from driving all day and decided to make a stop, buy bottled water and settle on a spot below an acacia tree, and gaze into the distance of the blue Mediterranean Sea in front of him. He stopped at the next village and bought bottled water from a shop, then decided to stop where the street came closest to the sea.

The constant lapping of the waves put him to sleep and he dreamt that he met a wonderful young woman, who took him along a deep cut gorge into the dark night lighting the path up with her magical lantern. She couldn't speak but she uttered some sounds, whenever they met along with dark shadows, which moved and growled like wild animals. She would utter some sounds that made them disappear into the ravines of the gorge at an instant. It was strange, but then she had taken his hand, he immediately trusted the elphin creature. She looked like a young girl and yet she had a figure of a boy, her athletic gait seemed strong and determined, but all the pieces of cotton veil wrapped around her body in numerous layers, rather accentuated her feminine nature.

He had encountered her in the twilight hour, when the spirits of the oncoming night greet their glowing sisters of sun-flooded days, who prepared for a restful night. That's when elphin of the moon-lit nights took over. Like all good spirits they brought sweet dreams to the children, looked-over the helpless and elderly, but all these duties behind them, they enjoyed most of all the company of poets. Some of these night spirits were especially dispatched from their domains of the endless sea, the floating clouds, and the mighty mountains, to look after the lonely travelling bards.

He thought that this gentle, delicate spirit, who reminded him of a young woman he had met in the village, as he bought some bottled water, just looked like her. In the fading daylight, her dusky eyes glimmered and her slim fingers clasped his strong hands. Whenever he thought tender thought about her, she pressed his hand. He wondered if he imagined that, but as soon as his heart warmed for her in a mental dialogue, her fingers clasped his hand. He enjoyed this game and as more he engaged with her in it, the more he felt that she came closer to him. She stopped and turned around to face him. She uttered voices and as his mind translated her words, he could not believe what he heard. She cited a poem from his *Cretan Journey:*

Myrto of my heart/ lithe as a breeze
From the sun-kissed sea/ a Muse
Out of the deep of the Nereid's Blue
She kisses my skin with tender words
With meandering curls of her smile.

His heart sang aloud as he moved his lips to his lyrics that touched him still deep within, and he asked her within his mind: "How come she knew it by heart?"

"By now, my dear poet, you should know it," she signalled back, "I am your Muse's spirit." His heart increased its beat. "So, you are Myrto?" She just smiled. "I'm happy you are here!" Her fingers pressed his hand.

"I'm surprised that you exist so real, well surreal, whatever I might call it, it doesn't matter. Important to me is the sound of words threaded together, to become a chain of pearls, a necklace of radiating beads that enhance the beauty of your smile." He pressed her hand gently and she stopped moving. Her lips close, he kissed her. Gently at first and as his blood started to boil, he kissed her with passion. Suddenly he felt the outlines of her body on his skin, as if this kiss had denuded them of their clothes. Then she stopped, moved away from his tight closeness and placed her finger to his lips. He tasted a waft of frangipani. He felt being in pure bliss and he wished he could make love to her. She must have read his thoughts and asked him to be more patient. "The night has not yet started, even if the stars are coming up above. We have to reach the top of the valley and emerge from the darkness of the gorge." He signalled back with his hand squeeze and she said: "I love your poem." He thanked her.

"Well, if you are Myrto's spirit, you must know that I fell in love with her, but she had restrictions in her heart to respond. I will call you Myrto from now on, as I have to give you a name. "Call me Yrto," she signalled and he agreed. "Tell me Yrto, why do we do this unusual trip?" Before she would answer, Yrto pulled him behind a rocky outcrop. The noise increased and became louder and sudden violent gusts blew through the upper part of the gorge, pulled at a tree with giant forceful hands, bringing down a huge fir tree that crashed past them, but a branch had scratched his shoulder as he ducked instinctively over Yrto to protect her. "Ouch," he said, as the wound started to burn.

"It's the dark powers of the night," Yrto said and kissed him. "They wanted to scare us, but you protected me, my dear poet." She hugged him closely. Yrto rose and checked his wound. "I will heal it," she said, "just stay here." When she returned, she rubbed some herbs into his wound and he felt the sudden sting. "It'll subside soon," she said. "We must continue, the village is not far any more. On a barren spot he stopped and turned without letting go of her hand. The dark sea lay far down, he could see the white crown of the waves and he realized they had climbed quite high already. Another gust of wind frightened him and he pulled Yrto close. She hugged him and signalled to him that it's all right. He kissed her. "Yrto darling," he mumbled. "Zeno, my poet," she replied, "the dark ghosts have no domain here at this height any longer. We have passed the strip of their dark, ruthless domain." She urged him on and they descended the last steep path to the village. A spicy scent wafted down. It smelled like chili, bit milder.

Yrto took a branch as a stick and she led the way, but battled with the undulated path. He asked her to let him use the stick, while she should light up the path. "Hold on to me, Yrto," he signalled her. "Yes," she responded, "we are already close." Suddenly he could see flickers of light through the foliage of trees and shrubs ahead of him, but still being higher up. Then he noticed a rail and he handed Yrto the stick, while he held on to the rail. "Let me go now first," Yrto said and took the lead. "It's better so, as they know me here." Well, he thought, people must be weary of strangers and he could not blame them. Red lights flickered.

Yrto emerged near the wooden deck of a square in midst of a giant tree with small fruit bunched in clusters. The huge tree was illuminated and he reached up to smell some fruit. He took a corn between his fingers and rubbed it. The smell of sweet pepper hit his nose. Suddenly the tree flashed as if a giant flame would leap from its crown. He felt a burn on his tongue and a rush of fire swept through his body. He missed Yrto's hand. "Yrto! Where are you?" He signalled, but he had no response. "I'm here Yrto!" He said aloud. Then somebody, like a shadow appeared out of the crown of the tree. "Can I help you?" The elphin figure of a woman stood next to him, looking just like her. "My name is Zeno," he said. She took his hand. "I am Yrto," she said and smiled lovingly. He was speechless for a moment and the dusky eyed woman continued: "Take a seat."

"Thank you," he replied.

"What would you like to drink?" He smile beguiled him. Just like Myrto, he thought. "I'll have an ouzo," he said, then added "a strong one." He sighed.

"I'll bring you a small bottle, cold water and ice."

"Thank you," he said and took his handkerchief from his pocket wiping his forehead. He had a fever, he was sure.

There are spirits in the mind, but there are hardly ghosts. Well, he wasn't sure any longer.

Yrto brought the drinks. She placed the tray on a free table and served some locals before she came to him.

"Just mix it to your taste, but be easy on it." She smiled.

"What would you like to eat? He studied the menu.

"Could I suggest something? He nodded, after he had looked into her eyes, whose dusky glimmer mesmerized his being, like a black panther hypnotizing his prey. He felt already being dead, eaten alive. "Yes," he said, as he finished her explanations in English. He understood it was a stew. "Who is the cook?"

"I am," she said and smiled, edging her hips onto him. He felt stirred. "What spice do you use?"

"This one," she pointed to the tree that hovered above him like a tropical plant painted by a surrealist artist.

"That's fantastic." He felt a wave of confidence starting to glow within him. With every sip of ouzo he felt better, elated, and happy to have been dreaming of Myrto and then guided by Yrto, to find out that the real Yrto ran a tavern here and spiced her food with pepper from a tropical tree.

He took the notebook from his sling bag and started to write down his experience. "If I don't do it now, it'll being forgotten by tomorrow," he mumbled. Yrto appeared. "Here we are, be careful, it's still hot." She bent down serving his plate of food nudging him again with her hip, and he noticed she had taken off her tee shirt and replaced it with a sleeveless sport top. Her nipples showed through the thin material as she bent down serving him a portion of olives to serve as a starter. "You are very..." He couldn't finish his sentence as she darted around serving customers. He gazed after her fascinated by her quick movements. Then he concentrated on his food.

He took his first bite. "Wow! This food was delicious," he mumbled. The more he dug into it, the more he heard the seductive voices of Yrto. She had turned from a spirit into flesh and blood, from a nymph of the moonlight into a woman with hot blood. He celebrated with ouzo and wrote his journal in trance. The customers had left and he noticed Yrto. "Did it taste good?"

"It was marvellous," he lauded her.

"Would you like coffee?"

"Yes."

"Follow me, as I have to close down here." He followed her to the small shop and coffee bar with a pizza oven and some pickled goods for sale. She let him sit close-by where she moved in and out. "Tell me how you came here, on foot?"

"Yes and a spirit of Yrto guided me."

"Well," she said, "that's interesting, I want to hear it."

"I'll tell you later, but do you have a room for the night?" He felt suddenly tired.

"Yes, I will show you just now, but first have your coffee in peace." She busied herself, brushing against him all the time, as she squeezed past his table. The room had been loaded with conserved local foodstuff for sale. He noticed that his whole body responded to her as she came close and brushed repeatedly at him, as if by accident. He looked at her and she smiled, then she starting to talk and asking about his trip and how he came to visit this particular village in the mountains. When he stood up to look at his cash he kept in his sling bag. She bumped into him and in a sudden want he kissed her. Like a wild cat she pushed herself into him.

"Yrto," he gasped and she kissed him back in return. "I want you!" The fire of the pepper burned in him and on him. It had flooded his whole body, his mind, and his being and on top of it all she leapt into him like a giant flame, starting a roaring fire. "Later," she whispered.

"Let's go to bed together," he said, but she left him suddenly and rushed outside. A man appeared and sat down on the bench adjoining the entrance to the inn. He saw them discussing something with empathy, waving their arms, gesticulating. He drank a whole jug of iced water, still burning inside. "The pepper love," he mused and smiled. Would she be available at night, or go to her boy-friend?

Suddenly she rushed into the small shop as the man had left in a hurry. "I will close soon and show you to your room," she said and smiled again. She had certainly raised his expectation for passionate lovemaking in him. As he had calmed down and felt balanced with a warm glow remaining in his inside, she locked the door, took his hand and asked him to follow her. He thought of Yrto as the spirit of Myrto, who had raised love in him. The moment she opened the door to the lowly lit room, he took her into his arms.

Fin.

About the author

Born in Eastern Austria, close to the Hungarian border, he witnessed as a young man the horrors of a nation's suppression, erupting in the Hungarian Revolution of 1956. He finished his education in art and architecture in Vienna, married and sailed for the Cape of Africa, an adventure that followed his childhood dreams. He had drawn African animals for his art classes, but the time had come to see them in their natural habitat.

Meeting a varied facet of people and cultures, working as a draughts-man in an engineering office, as an architect for a cultural centre, as a coordinator of craftsmen and professionals, he made good use of his language skills traveling throughout Southern Africa.

During a trip to Lesotho, a native artist showed him rock-paintings with their stark palimpsest outlines and with typified movements of animals and humans. It made a lasting impression on him and influenced his artistic work.

His vast collection of drawings and slides had been lost during a change of domiciles, but further studies of the art of the San-people reawakened his dormant artistic longing for expression of his art, filling sketchbooks with drawings and notepads with poetry and prose. While revisiting the capitals of Europe, he sensed the bond of art being borderless and free, reaching out across continents into the world.

During a visit to Greece, he was accepted into a circle of artists and poets, who encouraged him to continue his art and a friend introduced him to the works of famous Greek poets.

In South Africa, he joined he joined writing and poetry workshops of *Writers Write.* It was to open the floodgates of his creativity.

He decided to travel through Greece and visit its sites of antiquity, read-up on Classical mythology, and to enjoy translations of Greek poetry and prose.

He settled in 2023/14 in Klosterneuburg-Weidling. Poet Nikolaus Lenau is buried here. Franz Kafka had visited here. Their writings will always be an inspiration

Other Books by the author
(Available in the BoD-bookshop).

Acropolis – Book I Fervour

Athens Elegies – A Poet's Lament

Educating Pizzy - The Artist Evolves.

Fighting Stance – Triangulation in Love

King of Ice – A Poetic Legend

Spleen of Love – Zen & the Lake Moeris Adventure

The Fabricator - Life and Death of a Great Canvas

The Mill Below Owl Castle – Zol's Sentimental Education

Zora's Mistake – The Potential of a Hidden Error.